THE ETERNAL
TAO TE CHING

THE ETERNAL
TAO TE CHING

THE PHILOSOPHICAL MASTERWORK OF TAOISM
AND ITS RELEVANCE TODAY

A UNIQUELY AUTHENTIC TRANSLATION BASED ON
THE MEANINGS OF THE ANCIENT CHINESE CHARACTERS IN USE
WHEN THE TAOIST CLASSIC WAS WRITTEN

WITH PHOTOGRAPHS BY THE AUTHOR

BENJAMIN HOFF

ABRAMS, NEW YORK

This book is dedicated to Dr. Yi Wu, whose research and writings on the *Tao Te Ching* and Chinese philosophy were invaluable to me in the preparation of this volume; also to my two principal Taoist teachers, David Cheng and Dr. Yuet Sun Chan; and to my first and foremost teacher, *Ti Hsüan Tao*—Valley Spirit, Mysterious Female, Mother of the Ten Thousand Things.

B.H.

There existed something hazy and whirling,
completed before heaven-and-earth's beginning.
In *silence* and *emptiness*, it stood alone and
unchanging. In cycles it moved, but did not
wear down. It could be considered as being
The Mother of All Under Heaven. I do not know
its name. To designate it, I call it *The Way*.

FROM CHAPTER TWENTY-FIVE OF THE *TAO TE CHING*

CONTENTS

INTRODUCTION: THE AGELESS WISDOM OF A LONG-OBSCURED MASTERPIECE

ALL GREAT SPIRITUAL TEACHINGS, it would seem, are founded by complex minds driven by the desire for simplicity—minds that observe and reflect on deep, complicated matters, reduce them to their vital components, and then communicate these in ways that are easily understood by others. But after the founders are gone, the followers, those of simpler minds, complicate things.

The author of the *Tao Te Ching* streamlined the folk religion of China down to its foundation (eliminating its gods and goddesses) and rebuilt it as a man-in-nature philosophy, incorporating his advanced spiritual, philosophical, social, and political ideas. He wrote it down in the simplest terms, apparently without signing his name to his work—a fitting "signature" to a philosophy of non-egotism.

And then his readers complicated what he'd created. They altered his writing according to their own ideas, egos, and misunderstandings. They used his expressions to justify beliefs, attitudes, and behaviors quite different from those he'd advocated. They interpreted his philosophy according to those of later writers. They obscured his meanings with convoluted, twisting-and-turning commentaries and arguments . . .

And yet, visible here and there through all of that like sunlight in fog—concealed in *that* passage but revealed in *this* one—the long-hidden meanings and simplicity have remained. They are what I set out to retrieve.

Ever since its creation, the *Tao Te Ching* has stood alone among the world's writings. There was nothing like it before it appeared; there is nothing like it even now. Unlike a good deal of Chinese writing, old and new, it makes no reference to specific individuals or events, whether of the then-past or the then-present. It is not historical, not classical; its world is the world of *now*. Despite having been written around 2,400 years ago, it has not grown dated. One can get an idea of how extraordinarily modern it must have seemed to the Chinese of the far-distant past by reading the by-now-antiquated writings of the Confucianists. It is modern still, because it is timeless. The problems and conflicts it mentions are those that exist today. The solutions it presents are solutions that can be applied today. It is as creative and unique in its view of the world as its author is creative and unique in his use of language.

In the two following introductory sections, the chapter translations, and my notes on the chapters, I hope that I have managed to make understandable passages that have for years puzzled readers, myself included. As for my modifications to the standard Wang Pi text and my occasional selections from other historic editions of the *Tao Te Ching*, I've done my best to understand the author's statements and intent, avoid distorting or detracting from them, and make *clarity* my goal.

I once was employed by a master restorer of valuable but damaged antique objects. In writing this book, this literary and philosophical restoration project, I followed the principles he worked by: Thoroughly research the history of the object; remove all misguided, historically incorrect alterations and repairs; patch and fill where necessary; match the new work to the old so seamlessly that no one will detect a difference in treatment; honor the maker, his tools and materials, and his design; honor the tradition that has formed around the object over the years—but only if it honors the reality, not if it violates it; *the object is everything, misconceptions about it are nothing*. Good principles, I believe.

I like to think of this project as a partnership between myself and someone of another time, another place, and another language—someone with whom, despite those intimidating differences and distances, I seem to resonate. I have no illusion about which partner accomplished a *great* work. Sometime between 475 BCE and 300 BCE, apparently, he created something the likes of which had never before existed. In so doing, he gave to the world—seemingly that of the Warring States period of the Chou Dynasty—what it desperately needed. Today's Warring Nations world desperately needs it, too, as does the besieged, endangered world of nature, including the species known as Homo sapiens. After all, as the *Tao Te Ching* shows, the world of nature and the world of humanity are the same world.

For being an unprecedented, unequalled advocate for that world that I've loved since early childhood, and for enriching my life with his *Tao Te Ching*, I am grateful to the author far beyond my ability to express.

CRYPTIC WRITING, HIDDEN DRAGON

THE CHINESE SPIRITUAL TEACHING known as Taoism ("daoism") has two ages-old traditional forms: *tao-chiao*, the colorful and complex native religion, and *tao-chia*, the philosophical (no deified human beings) form that preceded the religion. This book is concerned with the philosophical form.

Philosophical Taoism was brought into existence by a written work that eventually became known as the *Tao Te Ching* ("dao dehr jeeng"), the "Way Virtue Classic." According to legend, this first and foremost Taoist classic was composed around 500 BCE by a former record keeper in the royal library at Loyang. But, as I explain later, the legendary claims don't match reality.

The verses of the *Tao Te Ching* look, and are, different from other Chinese writings, old and new. At first glance, they seem very simple—some look like children's rhymes, and many make use of rhyme intervals, rather like advertising jingles. Until the Communists took control of China and did their best to destroy Taoism—and Taoists—the verses of the *Tao Te Ching* were chanted in schools as a way to teach and learn the philosophical classic. But their simple, childlike appearance is deceptive.

Behind the simplicity of the statements in the *Tao Te Ching* lies a profound depth of thought. If philosophical Taoism were a religion, the *Tao Te Ching* would be its holy book. But the *Way Virtue Classic* covers more territory than any holy book I've encountered: It is mystical; it is practical; it is philosophical; it is spiritual; it is individual-oriented; it is society-oriented; it is political; it is ecological; it is simple; it is sophisticated; it is entertaining; it is deep. Some might call its Taoism a *system*—but one unlike the stiff, heavy-handed system of Confucianism. A Taoist might more accurately call it *fluid systems determined by circumstances*.

Although there are a great many English-language translations of the *Tao Te Ching* in existence, in reality they are by necessity interpretations, as is this one.

One reason for this is that the Chinese language is so strikingly different from the English language that for the most part a direct translation would itself need a translation—that is, an interpretation of the translation—in order to be intelligible. Another reason is that the author does not consistently use Chinese characters in what would today be considered the classical manner. In some places, he plays fast and loose with them, as though making up a language of his own. Chinese writing could be called a sort of shorthand. But the author often uses characters as a cryptic, minimalist shorthand, and sometimes uses them in the most basic pictographic ways. All of which makes the verse collection a puzzle as well as a work of literature. Deciphering the *Way Virtue Classic* is rather like finding one's way through a complex maze: With many of the characters, the translator/interpreter has a variety of meanings to choose from, each of which can result in progress or lead to an impasse. And there are other difficulties:

Over the centuries, Chinese scholars copying the *Tao Te Ching* sometimes inserted their own thoughts or other material into the text. Lazy, sloppy, or inadequately educated copyists introduced many errors—some very obvious, others less so. And, as explained in "Ancient Pictures, Ghostly Voices," the post-*Tao Te Ching* advent of the writing brush brought about frequent, sometimes extreme alterations to the meanings of the characters in use when the work was written. Consequently, for accuracy and fairness to the author, a translator/interpreter needs to research and use the *original* meanings, not merely translate from the more modern brush characters or translate the ancient characters into writing-brush characters and use *their* meanings.

As far as I can determine from the wording choices in all of the English-language editions in my extensive collection of *Tao Te Ching*s, I am the first English-language translator/interpreter—difficult though it is for me to understand why—to go by the meanings of the ancient characters. The original-meanings approach of this book may make it unique among *all* editions. I say this because I haven't heard or seen evidence of any edition in any country incorporating any of the meanings I've come across. If other interpreters had made any of those "game-changing" discoveries, I believe I would have heard or read about it.

The standard Wang Pi ("wahng bee") *Tao Te Ching* text used as an authoritative source by most scholars (and myself) contains what seems the smallest number of errors and tamperings—although in my opinion, it contains a great many—and reads the most consistently. Even so, a translator/interpreter ideally needs to be a linguistic code breaker as well as an author profiler in order to decipher statements and—a point about which I'm extremely particular—to determine which are most likely original and which are most likely the work of others.

At least in my opinion, the important question is not whether a translation/interpretation is perfectly accurate to any Chinese text, because no original has yet been found (all existing old texts are flawed copies) and perfect accuracy has therefore been rendered impossible. The important question is, or should be: *What is the author saying?* Being scholarly, vital though it is, only takes one so far in deciphering the unique work of writing known as the *Tao Te Ching*. In addition, one needs a working knowledge of Taoism coupled with *empathy*—the ability to read the author's intent. Following the traditional outside-looking-in scholarly approach to translating and interpreting the *Tao Te Ching* results in the sort of work that produces a sensible statement *here* but nonsense *there*.

Consider the first two statements made in the first "chapter" (section) of the *Tao Te Ching*. In classical Wade-Giles romanization, they read:

tao k'o tao fei ch'ang tao
ming k'o ming fei ch'ang ming

Tao in this case means "way," "path," or "road." *K'o* means "can be." It changes whatever noun follows it into a verb, so the second *tao* means "wayed." *Fei* is an emphatic "not, negative, opposition, contradiction" or "wrong." *Ch'ang* means "constant, consistent, unchanging" or "everlasting, eternal." *Ming* in this context means "name" or "title." So a basic translation would be:

way can be wayed *not* eternal way
name can be named *not* eternal name

Filling things out, we get:

[The] way [that] can be wayed [is] *not* [the] eternal way.
[The] name [that] can be named [is] *not* [the] eternal name.

The traditional English-language interpretation is:

The way that can be told is not the eternal Way.
The name that can be named is not the eternal Name.

But *tao k'o tao* does not translate as "way can be told"; it translates as "way can be wayed." "Wayed" would mean "way put into action" or "way done." How does one *do* a way, a path, or a road—by telling about it or by following it?

A more appropriate interpretation, I believe, would be:

The Way That Can Be Followed is not The Eternal Way.
The Name That Can Be Named is not The Eternal Name.

Isolated from the rest of the chapter, that interpretation may seem more confusing than the usual one, since the rest of the chapter can help one to realize what the two lines are referring to. Before I give an explanation of that wording, and in so doing explain why I believe that the usual interpretation misses the author's point, I'll say that, to me—and, from what I've read and heard, to many other people—the *usual* interpretation is confusing. After all, if the author truly believes that "The way that can be told is not the eternal Way," *why does he then proceed to tell about it in five thousand characters? What way is he then telling about—a false one?*

My explanation:

"The Way That Can Be Followed" is the *earthly world* aspect of the divine universal power. Personified by the author in Chapter Six as *ku shên*, "The Valley Spirit," it could be called The Way of Nature. It is visible in its actions and therein-revealed character, both of which the author throughout the *Tao Te Ching* urges rulers and subjects to emulate. Due to the impermanence of all physical life, The Way of Nature, The Valley Spirit, is here on loan, not for eternity. It will not *die* (Chapter Six), but it can *leave*.

"The Eternal Way" is the *spirit world* aspect of the divine universal power. The author in other chapters calls it *t'ien tao*, "The Way of Heaven." As Chapter Fourteen points out, it cannot be apprehended through the senses

(but it *can* be told about, as various chapters show); therefore it cannot be followed, cannot be emulated. It is everlasting.

"The Name That Can Be Named" is that of "The Way Than Can Be Followed": *ku shên*, "Valley Spirit," also known as *hsüan p'in*, "Mysterious Female."

"The Eternal Name" is that of "The Eternal Way." It cannot be heard by those in the physical realm any more than The Eternal Way can be seen, and therefore the author does not know it. "Way," he indicates in Chapter Twenty-Five, is a makeshift designation for that invisible, inaudible power—in Chinese terms, a *style (tzu)*, not a *name (ming)*.

In the first chapter, the author refers to The Way of Heaven as both "Without-Name" and "The Origin of Heaven and Earth"—the creator of the spirit world and the physical world. And he refers to what I call The Way of Nature as both "Has-Name" and "The Mother of the Ten Thousand Things," as it gives birth to all of Earth's beings. In various chapters, he describes the latter, "The Valley Spirit," as *feminine, elusive, mysterious*.

Those two aspects of the one universal power are often inclusively referred to in the *Tao Te Ching* as *tao*, "The Way." As indicated in Chapter One (in my translation), both are the same energy—*feminine* energy, as each *gave birth to* this or that. Unless the author specifies which aspect he's referring to, one has to know by context or, if that can't be done, by assuming that what he's saying applies to the whole energy, not to only one aspect of it.

Taoism is pictorially represented by the *t'ai chi* ("Supreme Ultimate") symbol, the circle divided by a curved line into a dark (*yin*) half and a light (*yang*) half, both of which The Way gave birth to. *Yin* is the power of the dark, the wet, the feminine; *yang* is the power of the light, the dry, the masculine. The *t'ai chi's* halves seem to be chasing each other around and around, representing the Taoist theme of *change*. The Way itself, however, does not change; it *effects* change. To better understand that last statement, one could visualize the *t'ai chi* as a slowly spinning mask, behind which in both the spirit realm and the earthly realm is The Way.

According to legend, the author of the *Tao Te Ching* was a man known by the shadowy appellation Lao-tzŭ ("lao-dzee," literally "Old Master"), designated in English as "Master Lao," a much-older contemporary, and philosophical opposite, of "Master K'ung"–K'ung Fu-tzŭ (551–479 BCE), known in the West as Confucius. Disgusted by the decline of the Chou Dynasty, the legend claims, Master Lao left his state of Ch'u, rode off into the semi-barbarian wastelands, and was never seen or heard from again. However, the legend continues, at Han-ku Pass he was recognized by the border guardian, who asked the master to write down his thoughts before he left so that others could be enlightened by them. The dashed-off result, the legend concludes, was what eventually became known as the *Tao Te Ching*.

The legend is very appealing, and adds to the aura of mystery surrounding the *Way Virtue Classic*. But there are some things wrong with it:

To begin with, there is no evidence that the Old Master ever existed, despite a now-much-doubted account of his life written in about 100 BCE by the Chinese historian Ssu-ma Ch'ien, an account that appears to have been based both on the legend and on what might be called local gossip. (Ssu-ma Ch'ien tells us that the Old Master's actual name was Li Erh, and that his posthumous honorific was Tan, giving him the name Li Tan. However, *li erh* means "long ears," and so does *tan*. "Li Tan" would mean "Long Ears Li." In Asia, long ears are considered a sign of good fortune, long life, and wisdom. So the historian, while claiming to give us actual names, gives us more generic titles or clichés.)

In contrast, there is no doubt whatsoever of the existence of the Old Master's alleged contemporary and philosophical opponent, Master K'ung, whose writings, editings of older works, and disciple-recorded sayings established the principles of Confucianism, and whose teachings were to become the state religion of China and strongly influence the lives of the Chinese, the Koreans, and the Japanese for more than two thousand years. Would it not be natural to suppose that "Master Lao," the alleged founder of Taoism, the second-most-influential philosophy of China, would have left some proof of his existence, aside from a collection of brief verses?

Also highly suspect is the claim that that collection of verses was hastily written. A careful reading of the profound statements of the *Tao Te Ching* should be enough to create doubt in the legendary explanation of their creation.

The possibly 85 percent of the *Tao Te Ching* that I as a writer consider the work of one mind was, I believe, composed at leisure by a

perfectionist—which can be deduced from the philosophical depth of its statements, the skill of their structuring, the well-thought-out and sometimes unusual choices of characters to express something extra-simply and efficiently, and the carefully worked-out rhythms and rhyme intervals throughout. Writing of that caliber cannot be hurried.

According to several scholars, the *Tao Te Ching*'s vocabulary and rhyme structure, as well as some of its ideas and phrasing, had not been in use before the Warring States period (475–221 BCE). Therefore, its author could not have been the legend's much-older contemporary of K'ung Fu-tzǔ.

Whenever in truth the author of the *Way Virtue Classic* wrote his extraordinary composition, why was he unknown? His existence as someone more substantial than a clichéd, fictional-seeming character with a generic non-name only became "verified" through a questionable, long-after-the-fact "history" based on hearsay that had accumulated over the years about the "Old Master." (Or about *some* old master, or old *masters*. There have been, and there are still, plenty of old masters in China.) The alleged author's alleged younger contemporary and rival, Master K'ung, spent his days being ignored and dismissed by the rulers he tried to influence—only after his death did his government-reform principles and system begin to gain powerful support—yet a good deal is known about him. When he died, he had approximately three thousand disciples, rejected though his teachings had been. One would have to believe that Taoism's founder had *none*. He seems to have had *no school, no followers. No one apparently even knew his name.* Was the second-most-popular philosophy in Chinese history—and the most popular Chinese philosophy in the West—created by an invisible man?

When I consider the statements made in the *Tao Te Ching*, translated according to the character-meanings in use at the time of their composition, the bitter, disillusioned Old Master of the legend fades away and is replaced by a young man very familiar with the writings, attitudes, and practices of the Confucianists—a young man who wants major changes made to the nation, but not the sort advocated by Confucianism. A highly educated literary genius with exceptional social awareness, a man of noble birth, he disdains the learning for the sake of accumulating ordinary knowledge that Confucianism advocates. Instead, he favors learning that will enable *changes* to be made—changes to improve the life of the individual and create a government responsive to and responsible for all the people—matters that will over the succeeding centuries prove to be largely neglected by China's Confucian system of government, one that forces the individual and the masses to honor and support the hierarchy of power, not the other way around.

Rather than be a traditional scholar writing philosophical musings and commentaries, this more ambitious scholar wants to simplify and "repackage" the ages-old folk religion of China as part of a spiritual and social philosophy. He wants to move it forward, and to make it politically viable—a force to be reckoned with, a movement of and for the people rather than of and for the wealthy and powerful. Although he has a mind older than its years, he has a young man's "fire" and impatience. He also has a strange, hidden sadness.

There is danger around him—possibly because to acknowledge his authorship would injure the honor of a noble family name, a high standing in society, or a scholarly reputation—and the situation forces him to keep silent.

There is another possible reason for the author disguising his identity, involving another sort of danger, that I came to increasingly believe in as I progressed through the chapter translations. Rather than give that reason here, I decided to let readers discover it step by step, as I did, as they read my notes on the translations. It completely changed my understanding of the *Tao Te Ching*. It may well do the same for others.

This young man, for some very strong and frustrating reason, cannot speak out directly or reveal his identity. So he surreptitiously records his principles, criticisms, and recommendations in writing (a Chinese tradition) and (another Chinese tradition) "puts on a beard"—he attributes his writings to a nebulous "Old Master." Doing so not only hides his identity, it also— intentionally or not—helps to ensure that his verses will be honored and his philosophy put into practice. Why will they be? Because China, until very recently, revered the old and undervalued the new, and the young.

Our American society, which is brand-new compared to China's, undervalues the old and reveres the new, even though the new is at best unproven and is at worst dangerous. So it is difficult for the culture of America or that of the West in general, both of which are young compared to China's, to understand the practice of "aging" a literary or pictorial work, or its creator, such as has long been carried out in the East.

In order to better grasp the advantages of that practice in the case of the *Tao Te Ching*:

Imagine a traditional Chinese play in which a young man, a scholar who has not yet passed his examinations, disguises himself as an old man, a teacher, in order to court a beautiful young woman watched over by her suspicious, curmudgeonly father—who, if he were to see and catch the young man, would have him severely beaten. But the young man is smarter than the older one, and with a false beard, old clothing, and a stooped posture, he gets past him, to the audience's amusement.

Replace the beautiful young woman in that plot with those able to read the ancient Chinese pictographic characters—which, to an extent, even the illiterate could do, as the characters were much clearer "pictures" than were later made with the writing brush—and replace the suspicious, curmudgeonly father with another threat (although that suspicious, curmudgeonly father may yet prove close to the truth) and you'll have the picture I by now have. What better disguising tactic could a young man carry out—a young man in, perhaps, a sensitive social position—than the tactic of the beard?

Whoever the author of the *Tao Te Ching* may have been by name, he most certainly was, as an interpreter of the *Way Virtue Classic* once wrote, "a man who liked to keep himself unknown." But you can know him. Read what he reveals about himself, and the world he lives in. You'll find him there.

ANCIENT PICTURES, GHOSTLY VOICES

TO HELP READERS UNDERSTAND my approach to deciphering the *Tao Te Ching*, I thought it best to give some background on the Chinese characters in use at the time the *Way Virtue Classic* was written, as well as on the evolution of their classical (brush-written) descendants.

So, first of all, when was the *Tao Te Ching* written? In the Warring States period, I believe, for reasons already given and by the wording of certain chapters. That gives a starting date of 475 BCE for the segment of time in which the work was probably written. The closing date, so far, is indicated in the following words by Red Pine (the pen name of Bill Porter) in his *Lao-tzu's Taoteching* (Copper Canyon Press, Port Townsend, 2009):

> In 1993, three bundles of thin bamboo slats containing selections of *Taoteching* verses were unearthed in a tomb near the village of Kuotien/Guodian in Hopei province. The tomb belonged to the tutor of the crown prince of the ancient state of Ch'u, and the bundles were probably used for different levels of instruction. Since these newly discovered copies have been dated to 300 BCE, give or take a decade or two, they constitute by far our earliest version of the *Taoteching*. . . . However . . . the Kuotien copies . . . don't include the entire eighty-one-verse text, and they rarely include the entire text of the verses they quote. [They consist of thirty-one chapters, only sixteen of which are complete.] Sometimes, they quote no more than a line or two.

By appearances, then, the *Tao Te Ching* was written sometime between 475 BCE and around 300 BCE, giving a period of approximately 175 years. My estimate for the time of composition would be around 375 BCE, possibly earlier.

To make an analogy: Imagine tracking someone through the wilderness and eventually coming upon footprints fresh enough to indicate that the individual you've been tracking is just over the next ridge. That's how close I believe we are to knowing when the *Way Virtue Classic* was written—and, possibly, who wrote it. So how would it have been written?

During the above-estimated period, the long-established characters of the Chinese language were inscribed on strips of bamboo (fortunately for archeologists, a very durable material), which were notched and strung together to form bundles, a number of which would make up the equivalent of a book. From the historian's point of view, the system was not foolproof: The strings could break, causing mix-ups in the order of passages, or losses of sections, and the intended order of bundles could be confused.

Writing at the time was carried out using what could be called an ancestor of today's felt-tip marker—a small-diameter reed or bamboo tube topped by a reservoir, down from which flowed (probably) black varnish by way of a narrow wick, the end of which formed the writing point. The great advantage of this marker was that it could write in any direction, creating thin-line circles, curves, and straight lines, and was therefore very precise, producing uniform and easily readable characters.

Later, around 200 BCE, a "pencil" was invented with a fibrous tip that would be dipped into the writing fluid and used to write on silk, which had not previously been possible. The "pencil" was faster to work with than the writing tube, but its characters were comparatively thick and crude, and its use produced some strange alterations. It was used at first for legal and official documents; then it began to be used by the public.

With the invention of paper by the Chinese sometime before the second century BCE, and the writing brush and ink somewhat later, the world of Chinese character writing changed dramatically.

New technology always seems to give with one hand and take away with the other: It creates benefits, but also drawbacks and dangers. Human beings have a tendency to focus on the benefits and ignore the drawbacks and dangers—until years later, when the latter can no longer be ignored. So it was with the invention of the writing brush.

The hairs of the writing brush could not form the circles, curves, and narrow lines made by the writing-tube device, and so could not draw the precise, easy-to-understand "pictures" that made up traditional pictographic characters. So the characters changed, haphazardly, across the nation. Lazy copyists altered the established characters with little if any apparent logic. If scribes could not duplicate with the brush the proper formation of characters, they would invent false ones. Writers "borrowed" characters to represent words formerly spoken but not written, and to replace difficult-to-write characters with easier-to-write ones of different meanings but similar sounds—or characters without even the element of sound in common. Meanings changed as illogically as the forms—new definitions were added, long-standing ones were cast aside.

According to Dr. L. Wieger, S.J. in his book *Chinese Characters: Their Origin, Etymology, History, Classification, and Signification* (a 1965 reprint of the 1927 edition, Dover Publications, New York):

> These *chia-chieh* [mistakes, literally "false/borrowed"] are the very reason why the interpretation of the Chinese characters, which was primitively simple and easy, became so intricate and so difficult. They obscure many texts, fill up the lexicons, overburden the memory, and exasperate the students. These sad results spring not from a vice inherent to the Chinese characters, but from their antiquity and from the carelessness of their successive keepers.

The highly educated Chinese were no help in combatting the breakdown of the written language. Caught up in the growing excitement over the writing brush's potential for expressing individuality, they created "running" scripts and other eccentricities of outstanding personality expression but mediocre or nonexistent *communicative* expression, producing an early Chinese literary equivalent of the sort of art that has abandoned meaning and representation and instead focuses on expressive brushwork. By the year 1 CE, according to one book of classical Chinese characters, "a man believed himself dishonored if he wrote in a legible way." The writing brush, the highly acclaimed new tool of communication, was not improving communication; it was wrecking it.

There was another factor behind the mistakes and inconsistencies in the various copyist-written versions of the *Tao Te Ching*. Long before that work apparently was written, Master K'ung complained of the decline he had witnessed over the years in the skills and knowledge of professional scribes.

And during the subsequent Warring States period, incessant fighting and accompanying social upheavals destroyed schools and otherwise disrupted the education of those being trained as scribes. So when the "pencil" and then the writing brush began to be used, the centuries-long weakening of the education of scribes made the situation a great deal worse than it otherwise might have been.

In around 120 CE was published the *Shuo Wên Chieh Tzŭ*, a posthumous work by the renowned scholar and "father of Chinese archeology," Hsü Shên (Hsü Shu-chung). A systematic collection of 10,516 of the original (ancient) characters, the *Shuo Wên* had been created to present scholars with the authentic, long-established forms and meanings to help ensure that the brush-written characters would be based more on historical reality and widely understandable uniformity and less on fancies, ignorance, and laziness.

Publication of the *Shuo Wên* inspired archeological research that uncovered more of the ancient characters. It also inspired studies analyzing and explaining them, resulting in enlarged, annotated editions of the original work.

For more than 1,800 years, one edition or another of the *Shuo Wên* has been claimed—sometimes justifiably, sometimes not—as an information source by publishers of Chinese dictionaries, including the analytical dictionaries of classical and ancient Chinese characters that I consulted in the preparation of this book.

However, that's not to say that every original meaning has been recovered. And, as Dr. Wieger has pointed out, a good deal of the damage to the ages-old forms and meanings of Chinese characters has not been corrected. Consequently, as I soon came to realize, I was not going to learn the original meanings of passages in the 2,400-year-old *Tao Te Ching* simply by relying on the classical (brush-written) character definitions, as other translators/ interpreters seem by their word choices to have done.

Examining the ancient characters helped me to better understand the definitions, or to choose which definition of several would be the most appropriate. It helped me to understand how Chinese characters originally worked, how their creators' minds worked, and how the author's mind worked. It helped me to determine if a passage was the product of another writer's mind. Often, meanings hidden in or destroyed by the brush-written characters were revealed in the simple pictures of the ancient ones.

Reading descriptions of the brush characters in books analyzing the Chinese written language, I encountered editorial comments such as: "A misrendering of . . ."; "A stupid mistake"; "The modern character is a fanciful deformation made by the scribes"; "A nonsensical alteration of. . . ."; and so on. Not long after I'd begun to translate passages of the *Way Virtue Classic* by researching the ancient meanings, I found myself agreeing with the attitude behind such comments. My own attitude became: A mistake is a mistake, and whenever I encounter one in the text, I will do what I can to fix it. The *Tao Te Ching* deserves no less than that.

As I soon discovered, there were three eras of text-copying mistakes to be dealt with. Those of the writing-tube era concerned the accidental substitution of similar characters of different meanings, or the mistaken reading of one character for another—for example, the apparent confusion of *chung* with then-nearly-identical *yung*, described in my notes for Chapter Four. The era of transition from the writing tube to the writing brush brought mistakes in meaning caused by the appropriation of characters to express meanings not originally intended—for example, the "borrowing" of the ancient character *yüeh* (in its brush-written form renamed *tui*), which retained its "picture" but completely changed its meanings, described in my notes for Chapter Fifty-Two. The writing-brush era added mistakes caused by sloppiness in the use of the brush—for example, described in my notes for Chapter Twenty, what I concluded was the accidental transformation of the important-to-understanding brush character *pi* in that chapter's text into the similar-looking but nonsensical-in-that-context *mên* by a copyist leaving out one stroke.

In addition to the above and various other mistakes, such as the frequent omission of characters, were many tamperings with the text over the centuries: "clever" insertions made by a number of individuals (which, clever or not, didn't fit the context or the author's style); the seeming elimination of important characters by copyists who misunderstood what was being said—which meant that I needed to deduce what the eliminated characters had been saying and express what appeared to be the author's intended meanings; as well as other muddy-the-water meddlings described in my chapter notes.

To prevent any misunderstanding: I didn't start out as a traditional scholar of the *Tao Te Ching*. The deeper I looked into the writing of that creative masterpiece, the less like a traditional scholar I became. I tend to carry out extensive research on anything that interests me, and because I'm a speed reader, I can cover a lot of territory in a relatively short amount of time. The time involved in this case was a very intense six-and-a-half years. In contrast, some Chinese and Western scholars have spent most of their lives studying the *Way Virtue Classic*. My approach to translating and interpreting it was not that of a scholar in the usual sense but more that of: (a) a writer, (b) the cryptanalyst I once aspired to be, and (c) a Taoist.

As a writer, I chose to base my interpretation of the *Way Virtue Classic* primarily on the standard Wang Pi text which, despite its flaws, is the best, most literary text available—the strongest framework on which to assemble a translation. Some very knowledgeable scholars have chosen to pick *this* character or passage from *this* text, *that* character or passage from *that* text, and so on, and then piece it all together. But the result in each case that I've seen is a sort of literary patchwork quilt. Others have focused intently on the individual characters but, it would seem, much less intently on what they are saying in sequence—or on the idea that they ought to be saying something coherent—and don't seem particularly bothered when a string of characters makes little, if any, sense. But translating the characters isn't enough. Figuring out what the characters were originally being used to communicate needs to be the point of the whole process—and that figuring depends to a large extent on an understanding of the character of the author.

Reading scholarly interpretations and analyses of the *Tao Te Ching* for years and then working on my own interpretation and analysis has convinced me that it takes a writer to "read" a writer and to understand the point of his writing when meddlers have tampered with his text. The matter of whether that conclusion is due to professional conceit or to professional literary meticulousness I will leave for readers of this edition to judge for themselves.

Regarding "the cryptanalyst I once aspired to be": In my childhood and adolescence, I was fascinated by codes and ciphers and spent a good deal of time reading codebreaker books such as Herbert Yardley's *The American Black Chamber* and working to create an unbreakable cipher. For a while, I intended to be an FBI cryptanalyst, or someone of the sort. Instead, I went on to other matters and forgot about "black chambers" (decrypting labs) and the FBI. But this project started the cryptanalyst part of my brain working again. I found myself treating the Chinese characters as codes (words-substitutes symbols) and treating the text's strings of characters as encrypted messages—an approach that, due to the originally pictographic nature of the Chinese written language, proved to be extremely helpful.

THE CHAPTERS:
ALL UNDER HEAVEN

TO ONE DEGREE OR ANOTHER, all English-language versions of the *Tao Te Ching* that I've read are what I would call *summarizing* interpretations—they paraphrase statements to present the general idea of what's being said. In contrast, the following version is a character-by-character interpretation that uses each character's meaning as the author used it—as a stepping-stone to understanding. Sometimes I left out a character because it seemed awkward or redundant in translation, not appropriate to the context, of suspicious origin, or for some other reason. Occasionally I deleted a passage—which one, and why, I specify in the notes for each chapter—or added a sentence or two for clarification, which I also address in the chapter notes. Whenever necessary, I "translated" Chinese character order into English word order. And I of course added words to the bare-bones translations to Anglicize what the author is saying in his shorthand-like Chinese. I omitted five chapters traditionally included because, as my notes on those chapters explain, I concluded that they were written by other authors.

The difference between a summarizing interpretation and a character-by-character interpretation can be demonstrated by the following exaggerated version of interpreted conversations I've overheard:

Imagine Party A asking a question, through an interpreter, of Party B. Party B responds to the interpreter with a five-sentence answer. The interpreter turns to Party A and summarizes: "He says, 'Yes, that's true.'" Wouldn't you like to know what's been left out? I always do. And I thought that readers of this book would like to know that, too.

The chapters (sections) of the *Tao Te Ching* are herein designated by their traditional numbers, as well as by titles of my own devising.

1.

THE WAY

The Way That Can Be Followed
Is not The Eternal Way.
The Name That Can Be Named
Is not The Eternal Name.

Without-Name is The Origin
Of Heaven and Earth.
Has-Name is The Mother
Of Every Earthly Being.

Consistently desire Without-Form
In order to study its mysteries.
Consistently desire Has-Form
In order to study its frontiers.

The previous two are the same energy,
But have different designations.
When those are joined, that is called
Growing darkness—
Darkness of ever-increasing darkness;
Many-mysteries' gateway.

2.

OPPOSITES
THE WISE

Under heaven, all know *goodness*—
It acts as goodness,
Then *evil* declines.
All know *harmony*—
It acts as harmony,
Then *dissonance* declines.

Existence and *non-existence*
Produce each other;
Difficult and *easy* complete each other;
Long and *short* clarify each other;
High and *low* rely on each other.

The wise exist in without-overdoing
Occupations;
They put into practice no-word
Teachings.
Why?
The ten thousand things act
Without speaking,
Produce without possessing,
Do without depending,
Achieve without lingering.
Only they do not reside in their
Achievements—
And because of that, they are not sorry
To leave them.

3.

NO DESIRE,
NO CONTENTION

Not elevating the superior
Causes people to not contend.
Not placing high value
On difficult-to-acquire objects
Causes people to not act like robbers.
Not putting desirables on view
Causes people's hearts and minds
To not exist in turmoil.

Rightly and accordingly,
The wise man's governing
Empties the people's hearts and minds
Of that discontent
And fills their bellies with food.
It weakens their obstinacy
And strengthens their bones.
That consistently causes the people
To exist without fast talk
And without desire—
It causes the fast talkers to not dare
To take action.

"Do without doing"—
Manage without forcing.
Then nothing will not be governed.

4.

DEEP WATER

The Way swirls round and round
Like a whirlpool,
And at its center
It may seem to not be full.
It is like dark water whirling
At the bottom of an abyss.
It is The Ancestor of the
Ten Thousand Things.

It is like deep water—
Unknown, unfathomable,
Preserving itself,
Continuing to exist.
I know not whose descendant it is—
It predates the earliest image
Of a Supreme Ruler.

5.

Deleted—see the notes on this chapter

6.

THE VALLEY SPIRIT

The Valley Spirit does not die.
She is called *The Mysterious Female*.
Her gate is called *the connection*
Between heaven and earth.

Like down or cotton—soft, soft—
Yet strong and lasting as silken floss
Spinning, spinning, thin and long,
She continues on and on.

Use her power, and your work
Will not be hard.

7.

ABLE TO ENDURE

Heaven is eternal,
And earth lasts long.
Why are they able to endure?
Because they do not live for
Themselves.
That is what enables them
To live on and on.

The wise man follows their example:
He puts himself behind,
Yet he ends up first;
He exists beyond his body,
Yet his body is preserved.
Is it not because he is without
Self-interest
That he is therefore able to attain
What is in his best self-interest?

8.

SUPERIOR GOODNESS

Superior goodness is like water.
Water excels at benefitting the
Ten thousand things
And does not contend with them.
It flows to humble places
That many men detest.
Therefore it is close to The Way.

Only those who do not contend
Cause no evils.

Good dwellings have land.
Good minds have great depth.
Good unions have benevolence.
Good speeches have sincerity.
Good governments have healing.
Good writings have power.
Good beginnings have timeliness.

9.
EXCESS

Fill it full, the cup you hold—
Will that not then prove excessive?
Overthin the blade you file—
Will it protect for just a while?
Fill your hall with gold and jade—
Will you be able to keep it safe?
Gain wealth, acclaim, and arrogance—
Will they not harm you in abundance?

Achieve results, then back away—
That is heaven's way.

10.
EMBRACING THE ONE

Managing your earth-grounded spirit
And embracing The One,
Can you be free of distinction?
Opening and closing the gates of heaven,
Can you be like the female?
Focusing your life force
To become pliant and soft,
Can you be like an infant?
Cleaning the flaws from your deep vision,
Can you be without failings?
Experiencing brilliance and clarity in
Four directions,
Can you be freed from your striving?

11.

THE VALUE OF EMPTINESS

Fit thirty spokes together
With one hub,
In order to make a wheel.
In its emptiness—
The hole in its hub—
Can be found the wheel's
Usefulness.

Shape clay into a form,
In order to make a vessel.
In its emptiness—
The cavity inside of it—
Can be found the vessel's
Usefulness.

Chisel out doors and windows,
In order to make a house.
In its emptiness—
The openings in its walls—
Can be found the house's
Usefulness.

Therefore, form is employed
In order to make things clever;
Emptiness is employed
In order to make them useful.

12.
MORE IS LESS

The five colors
Make people lose their sight.
The five tones
Make people lose their hearing.
The five flavors
Make people lose their taste.
Excessive racing and chasing
Make people lose their minds.
Hard-to-get objects
Make people lose their way.

The wise man, for those reasons,
Acts for his stomach
And not for his eyes—
He attends to contentment
And not to desire.
He lets go of the latter
And takes hold of the former.

13.
ENTRUSTED WITH THE WORLD

Favor-then-disgrace occurs
If there is *fear*;
Honor-then-great-affliction occurs
If there is *self*.

How can I say that
Favor-then-disgrace occurs
If there is *fear*?
Favor causes one to fall
If one fears to receive it,
If one fears to lose it.

How can I say that
Honor-then-great-affliction occurs
If there is *self*?
One accordingly has great affliction
Because one has a self.
Once one is without a self,
What trouble can one have?

How does one lose *fear*?
By losing the self.
How does one lose *the self*?
By going beyond it.

One who values the use of the self
To act for the world
Can be at home in it.
One who loves to use the self
To act for the world
Can be entrusted with it.

14.

THE WAY OF HEAVEN

Looked for, it cannot be seen–
It is called *The Invisible*.
Listened for, it cannot be heard–
It is called *The Inaudible*.
Reached for, it cannot be grasped–
It is called *The Intangible*.
Those three aspects cannot be conveyed
Or examined–
They blend and become The One.

Above, it is not bright;
Below, it is not dark.
Meeting it, one cannot see its face;
Following it, one cannot see its back.
It stretches, stretches away,
That Which Cannot Be Named,
Going back again to Nothingness.

That description could be called
The form of Without-Form,
The image of Nothingness.
It could be called *obscure, uncertain*.

Hold to The Way of the Ancients
In order to manage today's existence.
To know its ancient beginning is called
Clarifying The Way.

15.

THE ANCIENT MASTERS
PATIENCE

The ancient masters
Penetrated the minute,
The subtle, the mysterious.
Their depth could not be verified—
Mere men were not capable of
Testing it,
So they were forced
To describe the masters
By their appearance:

Cautious, as if fording a stream
In winter;
Hesitant, as if in awe of their
Neighbors in four directions;
Serious, as if they were strangers,
Visitors, guests;
Mutable, like ice about to break up;
Honest, like trees in a thicket;
Vast, like deep ravines;
Opaque, like turbid water.

Who can transform murky water
By waiting calmly for it to
Slowly clear?
Who can produce peace
By over time causing it to
Gradually grow?

16.

RETURNING TO THE SOURCE

On my reaching absolute emptiness,
Maintaining constant stillness and
Silence,
The ten thousand things arise together
In my mind.
I consider them, examine them—
Once more the many beings grow and
Flourish . . .
Once more each returns to its Source.

Returning-to-The-Source is called
Stillness.
It is said to be *returning to life*.
Returning-to-life is called *constancy*.
To-know-constancy is called
Enlightenment.
To-not-know-constancy is an error
That creates misfortune.

Knowing constancy, one then reaches
Receptive.
Knowing receptive, one then reaches
Impartial.
Knowing impartial, one then reaches
Kingly.
Knowing kingly, one then reaches
Heavenly.
Knowing heavenly, one then reaches
The Way.
Knowing The Way, one then reaches
Long life,
Submersion of the self,
And *freedom from danger*.

17.

THE FINEST RULER

The finest ruler:
His people only know
They have him.
The second-best:
His people love and
Praise him.
The third-best:
His people fear him.
The fourth-best:
His people despise him.
He has insufficient faith
In *them*,
So they have no faith
In *him*.

A great ruler is thoughtful,
Far-seeing, and foreseeing.
He values words, and so
Keeps them to himself.
When he achieves merit,
When his work succeeds,
All of his people say
"We did it, by ourselves!"

18.

A GREAT FALSEHOOD

The Great Way has been abandoned—
We have Benevolence and Righteousness.
Clever Knowing has arisen—
We have a great falsehood.
Family Relations have lost their harmony—
We have Filial Piety and Maternal Affection.
The nation's household is in darkness
And disorder—
We have Loyal Ministers.

19.

SIMPLIFY

Eliminate Sage-Kings, discard Knowing–
The people will benefit in a hundred ways.
Eliminate Filial Piety, discard Maternal Affection–
The people will return to esteem-for-parents
And motherly love.
Eliminate cleverness, discard profit–
Robbers and thieves will cease to exist.

Those three suggestions of mine
May be considered mere strokes and lines–
Not enough in themselves, I find–
So I have made a place for more of their kind:

See the natural, embrace the simple.
Lessen selfishness, decrease desire.
Eliminate studiousness, have no anxiety.

20.

I ALONE

Many people are "smiley-smiley,"
As when enjoying the great feast
Or ascending the tower in spring.
I alone am "anchored and fastened,"
Showing no sign of emotion—
Like an infant, not yet a child—
"Lazy-lazy!" as if I have nowhere
To go.

Many people have all they need,
And more;
I alone appear abandoned—
Left behind, forgotten.
My mind is that of a simpleton:
"Chaos-chaos!"

The common people are "bright-bright";
I alone am "dim-dim."
The common people "look-look";
I alone am "hidden-hidden"—
Tranquil as the sea,
Constant as a high wind.

I alone differ from the rest—
And yet I appreciate being fed by
Our Mother.

21.
SOMETHING ELUSIVE

Only Hidden Virtue's features precisely follow
The Way.

The Way's actions are but something elusive,
Something obscure:
They are obscure, they are elusive;
They contain *image*.
They are elusive, they are obscure;
They contain *substance*.
They are deep, they are dark;
They contain *spirit*.
That spirit is supremely true;
It contains *sincerity*.
From ancient times until now
Its renown has not passed away,
Because we observe all of its greatness.
How do we know the features of its greatness?
By turning and looking.

22.
ADHERING TO THE ONE

There is an ancient saying
About adhering to The One:

"The deformed shall then be whole;
The crooked shall then be true;
The hollow shall then be full;
The worn-out shall then be new."

The wise man holds to The One,
Becoming a pattern for all
Under heaven.
By not displaying himself,
He makes himself shine;
By not being self-righteous,
He makes himself attractive.
By not punishing himself,
He enables himself to acquire merit;
By not pitying himself,
He enables himself to grow.
He does not contend,
So the world is unable
To give him any contention.

So as for the saying of the ancients,
"The deformed shall then be whole":
Are those empty words?
Be truly whole and return to them.

23.

SWIRLING WINDS, SWIFT RAIN

To speak sparingly is natural—
Swirling winds will not last through the
Morning;
Swift rain will not last all day.
What causes them? Heaven and earth.
Even if heaven and earth wish them to,
They will not be able to last for long—
And how much truer that is
For the windy jabbering of men!
So be one who follows and works with
The Way.

One who is of The Way has joined with The Way.
One who is of Virtue has joined with Virtue.
One who is of Error has joined with Error.

He who joins with The Way: The Way is truly
Glad to receive him.
He who joins with Virtue: Virtue is truly
Glad to receive him.
He who joins with Error: Error is truly
Glad to receive him.

24.

USELESS ACTION

He who rises on tiptoe
Cannot stand firm;
He who stands astride
Cannot move forward.
He who displays himself
Does not shine;
He who is self-righteous
Does not attract.
He who punishes himself
Will not have merit;
He who pities himself
Will not grow.

Those who work with The Way
Call these *excessive eating*
And *useless action*.
Everyone, perhaps, dislikes them.
So those who are with The Way
Do not dwell in them.

25.

IN THE SILENCE

Before the birth
Of heaven and earth,
A mixture formed;
Something was born.
It stood, alone
And changeless,
In the *silence*
And the *emptiness*.
It moved in cycles,
Spinning round;
Yet its energy
Did not run down.
All under heaven
Did it bring—
It is The Mother
Of Everything.
I do not know
Its name—
To designate it,
I call it *The Way*.
If I were forced
To give a word for it,
I would call it *great*.

What-I-Call-Great
Goes on and on.
What-I-Call-Ongoing
Reaches far beyond sight.
What-I-Call-Far-Reaching
Returns.

Man follows the earth,
The earth follows heaven,
Heaven follows The Way.
The Way follows its own
Nature.

26.

THE WISE PRINCE

Heaviness is the anchor of
Lightness.
Stillness is the sovereign of
Rashness.
Therefore, the wise prince,
When traveling all day,
Does not go far from his
Baggage-wagons.
Although he has honor and glory,
And he views and considers
Feasts and fine dwellings
As he goes on his way,
He, however, passes them by.

By what means could the lord
Of ten thousand warrior-wagons,
Under those circumstances,
Consider himself light under
Heaven?
If he were to behave lightly,
He would lose his anchor.
If he were to behave rashly,
He would lose his sovereign.

27.

SUBTLETY

A skilled walker leaves no tracks.
A skilled speaker makes no mistakes.
A skilled counter uses no devices.
A skilled gate-securer requires no
Fixed crossbar,
Yet the gate cannot be opened.
A skilled binder needs no cord,
Yet whatever is used cannot be
Loosened.
As with those subtle skills:

A wise man is always skilled
At assisting other people
So that none of them feels abandoned,
And at helping other beings
So that none of them feels cast aside.
This subtlety of the wise is called
Cloaking one's own light.

The skilled man is the unskilled man's
Master;
The unskilled man is the skilled man's
Material.
To not honor one's master
Or to not love one's material,
Even if one is clever,
Creates a great delusion.
That is called *struggling for the subtlety*.

28.

CONSTANT VIRTUE
NATURAL SIMPLICITY

Know the masculine;
Retain the feminine.
Be a mountain stream
To all under heaven.
Be a mountain stream
To all under heaven—
Constant Virtue
Will not leave you.
Return again to the
Infant state.

Know the brilliance;
Retain the shadow.
Be a pattern to all
Under heaven.
Be a pattern to all
Under heaven—
Your Constant Virtue
Will be free of excess.
Return again to The
Origin of Everything.

Know the honor;
Retain the humility.
Be a valley to all
Under heaven.
Be a valley to all
Under heaven—
Your Constant Virtue
Will then be complete.
Return again to Natural
Simplicity.

The Natural Simplicity of
Government
Can be broken up to form
Political utensils.
When the wise man uses it
In its wholeness,
He will then prove to be
An excellent official.
So a great political system
Is one that has not been
Reduced to fragments.

29.

SACRED VESSEL

If you possess a desire
To take hold of the world
And *manage* it,
I see that you will not get
What you wanted.
The world is a sacred vessel—
You will not get away with
Tampering with it.
Whoever tampers with it
Will ruin it.
Whoever grasps it
Will lose it.

Therefore, the wise
Discard the excessive,
Discard the extravagant,
Discard the extreme.

30.

THORNS AND BRAMBLES

One who works with The Way
To assist a lord of men
Does not use military might.
Military affairs are fond of
Rebounding and retaliation.
Where troops have encamped,
Thorns and brambles grow.
When a great army passes,
A lean year surely follows.

The good attain the outcome
Desired, then stop.
They do not use violence
In order to gain power.
They achieve results,
But do not destroy.
They achieve results,
But do not force.
They achieve results,
But not in excess.
They achieve results,
But are not arrogant.
They achieve results,
But do not boast.

31.

WEAPONS AND WAR

Man's fine weapons are not utensils of
Good fortune.
All beings, perhaps, detest them.
So followers of The Way do not
Live with them.

Those who use weapons are themselves
Not good fortune's utensils—
They are not the tools of a princely master.
When such a man cannot bring about
A resolution without them,
He then may choose to use them;
But a desire for peace and serenity
Is his highest motivation.

Conquest is not worthy of a gentleman.
Those who consider it such
Are those who take pleasure in killing.
Those who take pleasure in killing
As a consequence will not find it easy
To obtain what they want in the world.

In matters concerning good fortune,
The left side is honored;
In matters concerning ill fortune,
The right side is honored.
At home, the princely master accordingly
Seats the most highly honored on the left;
At war, he accordingly gives the highest
Honor to those on the right.
The army's second-in-command occupies
The left side;
The army's supreme commander occupies
The right.
It could therefore be said
That the positions of honor held in war
Are those held in the funeral rites.

When many have been slain in battle,
And are mourned by their kind
With sorrow and weeping,
Those who have won the battle
Need to accordingly consider their victory
As a funeral.

32.

WITHOUT TITLES

The Way is always
Without title, rank, or position.
Although its Natural Simplicity
Makes it seem small,
No one under heaven is capable
Of making it his subject.
If princes and kings were able
To guard it and protect it,
The ten thousand things would
Act as their guests.
Heaven and earth would notice,
And would unite to send sweet dew.
The people, without being commanded,
Would then behave as equals.

Since the beginning of systems,
Rules, and regulations,
We have had titles, ranks, and
Positions. In addition,
The titles, ranks, and positions
Have had *us*.
Those who hold on to wisdom
Stop.
By knowing to stop, they can
Avoid danger.

Compared to man's constrictive
Systems, rules, and regulations
And titles, ranks, and positions,
The Way's existence in this world
Is like a broad stream in a deep gorge
Running into a large river
Flowing to the sea.

33.
HE WHO . . .

He who understands others has brilliance;
He who understands himself has *enlightenment*.
He who conquers others has muscle;
He who conquers himself has *strength*.
He who increases his riches has wealth;
He who is content with enough has *abundance*.
He who moves forcefully has resolution;
He who stands his ground has *endurance*.

He who dies but does not lose presence has
Longevity.

34.
THE GREAT WAY

The Great Way flows everywhere—
It can go left, it can go right.
The ten thousand things
Rely on it, and flourish,
And do not refuse it.
It accomplishes deeds of
Excellence,
Yet does not have a title—
It clothes and feeds
The ten thousand things
And does not act their lord.
Constantly without desires,
It could be designated
Among the Small.
The ten thousand things
Belong to it, return to it—
Yet it does not act their lord.
It could be designated as being
Great.

Because it ultimately does not
Conduct itself as great,
It is therefore able to achieve
Its greatness.

35.

THE IMAGE OF NOTHINGNESS

Hold to the great image—
The image of *Nothingness*—
As all-under-heaven wanders by.
As it does, it will not disturb
The supreme peace and harmony.

Elsewhere, the sound of music
And the scent of delicacies
May make passing strangers stop;
But a description of The Way
Is tasteless,
For The Way has no flavor.
When one looks for it,
There is not enough to see.
When one listens for it,
There is not enough to hear.
When one makes use of it,
There is not enough to satiate.

36.

Deleted—see the notes on this chapter

37.

TRANQUILITY

The Way is constantly without
Striving,
And yet without *not-acting*.
If princes and kings were able
To guard it and protect it,
The ten thousand things
Would act to improve them.
Improved, if they still desired
To take aggressive action,
Their awakened consciousness
Would restrain them with
Without-Name's Natural Simplicity.
With Without-Name's simplicity,
Others also would be without
Desires,
Not-desiring with tranquility.
All under heaven would behave
Peacefully.

38.

VIRTUE AND PROPRIETY

High Virtue is not "Virtue";
Therefore it has Virtue.
Low Virtue does not lose "Virtue";
Therefore it is without Virtue.

High Virtue is without striving,
And is without reason to strive.
Low Virtue strives for Virtue,
And has reason to.
High Benevolence strives for it,
But is without reason to strive.
High Righteousness strives for it,
And has reason to.
High Propriety strives for it,
And negatively it responds—
So High Propriety grabs it by the arm,
And throws it away.

We lose The Way,
And then we have Virtue.
We lose Virtue,
And then we have Benevolence.
We lose Benevolence,
And then we have Righteousness.
We lose Righteousness,
And then we have Propriety.

The man of Propriety:
His Loyalty and Sincerity are
Meager and thin—
He is confusion's leader.
One who prejudges a situation
By the rules of Propriety
Is a flower, an ornament, of
The Way,
And stupidity's beginning.

The great, revered men dwell
In the thick, not in the thin;
They reside in the substantial,
Not in the flowery.
They discard the latter
And take hold of the former.

39.

THESE ACQUIRED THE ONE
TAKING THE LOWLY AS THE ROOT

In ancient times, these acquired
The One:
The sky, in order to be pure;
The earth, in order to be serene;
The spirits of nature, in order
To be energetic;
The valleys, in order to be
Abundant;
The ten thousand things, in order
To be productive;
The princes and kings, in order
To be fortunate under heaven.
The One brought all of that about.

The sky, without purity,
Would be fearful of dispersing.
The earth, without serenity,
Would be fearful of erupting.
The nature spirits, without energy,
Would be fearful of ceasing.
The valleys, without abundance,
Would be fearful of depletion.
The ten thousand things,
Without productivity,
Would be fearful of perishing.
The princes and kings,
Without the honor of nobility,
Would be fearful of falling.

That which is honorable
Takes the lowly as its root;
That which is eminent
Takes the humble as its foundation.
That is why princes and kings,
Gaining through modesty,
Call themselves *orphaned*,
Solitary, and *poor*.
Is that not taking the lowly as
The root? Therefore:

Make your many-carriages attitude
A no-carriages attitude.
Do not desire to "shine-shine" like jade,
Or "clatter-clatter" like a stone necklace.

40.

RETURNING

Returning is the *motion* of The Way;
Tenderness is the *utilization* of The Way.

Under heaven, all things come forth
From Being;
Being came forth from Non-Being.

41.

HEARING OF THE WAY
THE WAY IS HIDDEN

The highest scholar,
Hearing of The Way,
Devotedly follows it.
The average scholar,
Hearing of The Way,
At first seems to retain it
Then seems to lose it.
The lowest scholar,
Hearing of The Way,
Loudly laughs at it.
If it were not laughed at
By such men,
It would not be sufficient
To be considered as being
The Way.

The Way is hidden,
Without a name.
Only that Nameless One
Kindly lends itself to all
While, however, remaining
Perfectly whole, complete.

42.

ONE, TWO, AND THREE
LOSS AND GAIN
FORCEFUL AND UNBENDING

The Way gave birth to The One;
The One gave birth to The Two;
The Two gave birth to The Three;
The Three gave birth to the ten
Thousand things.

The ten thousand things
Carry The Dark on their backs
And carry The Light in their laps.
They rotate the two energies
In order to achieve harmony.

What people greatly dislike is being
Orphaned, insignificant, or worthless.
Yet kings and dukes,
When they show courtesy to others,
Refer to themselves with those words.
By diminishing themselves, they gain.
By increasing themselves, they lose.

What others teach, I will teach also:
Those who are forceful and unbending
Do not die natural deaths.
I will use that to be the father
Of my doctrine.

43.

WITHOUT EFFORT

The world's ultimate yielding softness
Quickly rides over
The world's ultimate unyielding hardness.
Without-Form enters without-openings.
Because of them, I know without-effort's
Advantages.

No-word teachings and without-effort benefits—
Under heaven, few grasp them.

44.

WHICH DO YOU LOVE MORE?

Your position or *your self*—which do you love more?
Your health or *your wealth*—which is more ample?
To acquire or *to lose*—which does more harm?

Too much love for rich things is without doubt
A great waste.
Too much stored-and-concealed is without doubt
A large loss.

If you know what is enough, you will not be
Disgraced.
If you know when to stop, you will not be
Endangered.
If you are able to adopt these principles,
You will grow for a long time.

45.

Deleted—see the notes on this chapter

46.

ENOUGH

When the nation works with The Way,
Rejected racing-horses pull manure carts.
When the nation works against The Way,
War-horses are bred in the grounds
Beyond the city.

No affliction is greater than to not know
The meaning of *enough*.
No fault is greater than to desire gain.
Those who know when enough is enough
Will always have enough.

47.

WITHOUT GOING

Without going out the door,
One can know of the ways of the world.
Without watching through the window,
One can perceive The Way of Heaven.
The farther away one travels,
The less one understands.

Rightly and accordingly, the wise:
Do not step out, yet they know;
Do not look out, yet they perceive;
Do not strive, yet they accomplish.

48.

DECREASE

To pursue study, increase every day.
To follow The Way, *decrease* every day.
Decrease, then again decrease,
In order to arrive at *without-striving*—
Without *striving*, yet without *not-acting*.

To take hold of the nation, always use
Without-busyness.
Reaching for it while holding busyness
Will not be sufficient.

49.

VIRTUE
THE WISE MAN

I am good to those who are good.
I am also good to those who are not good.
Virtue is goodness.
I am sincere to those who are sincere.
I am also sincere to those who are not sincere.
Virtue is sincerity.

The wise man has no set mind—
He adopts the people's minds as his own.
The wise man applies his powers and abilities
Under heaven—
Harmonious, harmonious he makes the world
By merging his mind with it.
The people all turn their ears and eyes
To the wise man—
They all are children to him.

50.

ONE IN TEN

From coming forth at birth
To entering the ground at death,
The foot soldiers of life are three in ten;
The foot soldiers of death are three in ten.
The lives of those who move to a
Death place are also three in ten.
As for these last three in ten,
For what reason do they move to a
Death place?
It is because they live lives
That grow too rich and sheltered.
As for the one in ten:

I have heard that those who are
Good at nurturing life
Can walk the land without meeting
A wild yak or tiger,
Can enter battle without
Armored covering or weapons.
With them, a yak has no place
To thrust its horns,
A tiger no place to put its claws,
A weapon no place to sink its blade.
What is the reason for that?
Such people survive because they have
No death place.

51.

THE TEN THOUSAND THINGS

The Way produces them,
Virtue feeds them,
Matter forms them,
Circumstances develop them.
Therefore, without exception,
The ten thousand things
Venerate The Way
And honor Virtue.
Their veneration of The Way
And their honoring of Virtue
Are not demanded of them,
But always are self-generated.

So The Way gives birth to them;
Virtue feeds them, grows them,
Rears them, strengthens them,
Watches over them, nourishes
And shelters them—
Producing but not possessing,
Acting on but not leaning on,
Growing but not controlling.

All of that is spoken of as
Deep Virtue.

52.

THE WORLD'S MOTHER

All under heaven had an origin,
Considered as being The World's Mother.
When you get acquainted with The Mother,
You will accordingly know her child.
When you know her child,
You will repeatedly protect The Mother.
To the end, your self will not be in danger.

Stop your pleasant words, shut your gate—
To the end, your self will not struggle.
Start your pleasant words, further your
Affairs—
To the end, your self will not be saved
From wrong.

Perceiving The Small is called *enlightenment*.
Protecting The Soft is called *strength*.
Employing The Great Mother's light
And repeatedly returning to her radiance
Without leaving your troubles behind
Is said to be merely *practicing* constancy.

53.

THE SHORTEST PATH

Supposing that I had a little
Glimmer of awareness,
I would travel only on
The Great Way,
Giving it the greatest respect.
The Great Way is very easy,
But the family is fond of
The shortest path.

The royal court is neglected.
The fields are full of weeds.
The granaries are empty.

Dressed in elegant colors,
Wearing sharp swords,
Overfull of drink and food,
Having a surplus of riches
And possessions,
These men are spoken of as
Rob-and-boasters.
It is clear that *they* are *not* of
The Way.

54.

CULTIVATE GROWTH

What is well-established
Will not be uprooted;
What is well-embraced
Will not be cast aside.

Cultivate growth in the self;
Then its Virtue will be ingrained.
Cultivate growth in the family;
Then its Virtue will overflow.
Cultivate growth in the village;
Then its Virtue will long endure.
Cultivate growth in the nation;
Then its Virtue will be abundant.
Cultivate growth in the world;
Then its Virtue will be universal.

Consider the self according to
The self.
Consider the family according to
The family.
Consider the village according to
The village.
Consider the nation according to
The nation.
Consider the world according to
The world.

55.

LIKE A BABY

One who is filled with Virtue's abundance
Can be compared to a newborn baby.
What qualities does a newborn baby have
That could invite such a comparison?
Wasps and scorpions do not sting him,
Venomous snakes do not bite him,
Ferocious animals do not seize him,
Birds of prey do not attack him.
His bones may be weak, his sinews soft,
But his grip is strong.
He does not yet know the union of male
And female,
And so acts in wholeness.
His essence is developing perfectly.
To the day's end he cries out,
But is not hoarse.
His harmony is growing toward perfection.

To-know-harmony is called *constancy*.
To-know-constancy is called *enlightenment*.
To-increase-one's-life is called *good fortune*.
To-send-energy-with-the-mind is called *power*.

Beings that grow too strong—
Too robust, too bulky, too inflexible—
As a rule consequently grow old too soon.
That is said to be *not The Way*.
Not-The-Way comes to an early end.

56.

DEEP UNITY

Those who know do not speak;
Those who speak do not know.

Stop your pleasant words,
Shut your gate.
Break off the pointed;
Untangle the disordered;
Harmonize with the light;
Join with the dust.
That is called *Deep Unity*.

Having attained that unity:

You will not be able to gain
Closeness from it;
You will not be able to gain
Distance.
You will not be able to receive
Profit from it;
You will not be able to receive
Injury.
You will not be able to acquire
Honor from it;
You will not be able to acquire
Disgrace.

But you will be valued
Under heaven.

57.

CAUSE AND EFFECT

Confucianists have a saying:
"By means of the upright
Govern the state."
Militarists have a saying:
"By means of the unexpected
Deploy military forces."
I have a saying:
By means of without-busyness
Hold on to the nation.
How can I know it is of value?
By stopping, turning, and looking:

The more fearsome prohibitions
There are under heaven,
The more complete is the poverty
Of the people.
The more there are of posted laws
And commands,
The more robbers and thieves exist.
The more sharp operators there are
Manipulating the people,
The more confusion we have
In the nation and the family.
The more men there are of cleverness
And cunning,
The more strange matters arise.

For those reasons, a wise ruler
Has said:

"I rule without forcing, and so
The people self-transform.
I love peace and stillness, and so
The people self-correct.
I act without busybodying, and so
The people self-enrich.
I live without desires, and so
The people self-simplify."

58.

Deleted—see the notes on
this chapter

59.

RESTRAINT

Governing people, serving heaven—
Are not both of them like practicing
Wise economy?

Only those of thrift-like restraint
Can be said to return early
To the childlike, uncluttered state.
This early return—call it
Weighty accumulation of Virtue.

One having accomplished that,
Then nothing cannot be subdued.
When nothing cannot be subdued,
Will not one know that that is the utmost?
Is it not by knowing that that is the utmost
That one can accordingly be capable
Of governing the nation?

Ruling with The Nation's Mother,
One can thereby long endure.
That is called *deep root, firm
Foundation*—
The way of long life and lasting
Vision.

60.

THE UNHAPPY DEAD

Governing a large nation
Is like cooking a small fish.

If the world were governed
In accordance with The Way,
The spirits of the unhappy dead
Would not have extensive power.
It is not that they would then
Not be powerful;
It is that their power
Would then *not injure* people.
And that is *not* because the
Extensive power of the unhappy
Dead *cannot* injure people.

The wise as well do not
Harm people, living or dead.
So then, under The Way,
Neither the wise nor the ghosts
Would hurt each other.
Virtue would bring them together
And restore harmony to the
Unhappy dead.

61.

ONE THAT LIES BELOW

A great state is one that lies below
The restless flow of movement—
All-under-heaven's crossings-swale,
All-under-heaven's female.

The female always uses peace and stillness
To overcome the male—
Using her serenity, she places herself
Below him.

In a similar way, a large state,
By placing itself below a smaller one,
Can accordingly gain the other;
And a small state, by placing itself below
A larger one,
Can accordingly gain the other.

In such a manner, someone can
Lower himself in order to gain.
Being lower, he will thereby attain
The advantage.

A large state desires to unite and
Feed people;
A small state desires to bring in and
Serve people—
So each of them obtains what it wants.

It is fitting for that which is great to
Lower itself.

62.
MYSTERIOUS SANCTUARY

The Way is the mysterious sanctuary
Of the ten thousand things—
The treasure of the good,
The protector of the bad.
Sweet words can buy and sell,
Respectful conduct can add to them,
But those do not redeem the bad—
Only The Way can do that.
So why have the bad rejected
Its assistance?

Considering all that,
On the day the Son of Heaven
Is established on the throne,
Or the three ministers of state
Are installed,
Even though your hands are filled
With a tablet disc of jade
And your carriage is to be pulled
By a splendid four-horse team,
It is better yet to rest where you are
And send instead The Ancient Way.

The reason why the ancestors
Valued The Way—what is it?
Is it not said that those who seek
Can obtain from it whatever they are
Searching for,
And that those who have done wrong
Can obtain from it forgiveness?
That is why it is valued under heaven.

63.

DO WITHOUT DOING

Do without *doing*,
Work without *working*,
Talk without *talking*.
Make small the large,
Make few the many,
Repay ill will with Virtue.

Resolve the difficult
Through the easy.
Achieve the great
Through the small.

The difficult work in this world
Must begin with the easy;
The great work in this world
Must begin with the small.
That is why the wise,
To the last,
Do not struggle for greatness—
And it is why they are able
To achieve it.

Those who promise lightly
Will be seldom believed—
What they see as very easy
Proves much more difficult.
The wise, however,
Treat work as difficult—
So they begin with the easiest
And smallest parts of it.
And to the end, they have
No difficulty.

64.

BEGINNINGS

The tranquil is easy to maintain;
The omen-free is easy to plan.
The brittle is easy to split;
The small is easy to break.
Act something through
Before it comes into being;
Oversee it thoroughly
Before it turns into chaos.

A tree one's arms can embrace
Begins with a minute grain of pollen.
A nine-story tower rises from
Three stones joined on the ground.
A three-hundred-mile journey
Starts on what is under one's foot.

One who forces something
Will destroy it;
One who grasps something
Will lose it.
Because of that:
The wise do not force,
So they do not destroy;
They do not grasp,
So they do not suffer loss.

The many, pursuing their projects,
Consistently almost succeed
But then founder.
If one is as cautious at the end of
An undertaking
As one was at the beginning,
Then that undertaking will not fail.

The wise desire *beyond-desiring*,
And so do not value objects
That are difficult to obtain.
They learn *beyond-studying*,
And so return to what the many
Have left behind.
In order to assist the inner light
Of the ten thousand beings,
They therefore do not act with
Violence.

65.

SIMPLICITY

The rulers of ancient times
Who were skilled at following The Way
Did so not *to enlighten* the people
But *to hold them to the state of simplicity*.
The people are growing difficult to govern
Because they are much too clever.
For that reason:

He who governs with cleverness
Is the despoiler of the state.
He who governs without cleverness
Is the benefactor of the state.

He who knows the previous two principles
Knows, moreover, to examine patterns.
To always know to examine patterns
Is what could be called *Profound Virtue*.

Profound Virtue is deep, far-reaching—
It enables all to turn back to simplicity,
And to thereby then regain the state of
Great cooperation.

66.

RULERS OF THE HUNDRED VALLEYS

The wide rivers and expansive lakes
Are able to be rulers of the hundred valleys
Because they are good at positioning themselves
In the lowest places.
That is what enables them to rule.

So those who want to rule the people
Must with their words be below them.
Those who want to lead the people
Must place themselves behind.

That is why the wise man,
When he eventually comes to rest
In a high position,
Does not make the people feel oppressed;
And why when he eventually comes to rest
In an advanced position
Does not make them feel slighted.
It is why all delight in him—
Why they push him forward
And never tire of him.

Because he does not contend,
The world is unable to give him
Any contention.

67.

THREE TREASURES

In this world, everyone says that
My way is noble—
It seems not like my father's.
That is, it is noble *because*
It seems not like my father's.
If it were like my father's for long,
It would be *small*, instead.

I have three treasures to hold
And protect:
The first is called *compassion*;
The second is called *economy*;
The third is called *not daring to be*
First in the world.

With compassion, one can be brave.
With economy, one can be expansive.
With not-daring-to-be-first-in-the-world,
One can become a leader of men.

To do without compassion,
But to practice bravery;
To do without economy,
But to practice great expansion;
To do without walking behind,
But to practice being first—
All of that is fatal.

Those who fight with compassion
Accordingly excel.
Those who protect with compassion
Accordingly gain strength.
Heaven will act to save them, and
Will with compassion guard them.

68.
NOT CONTENDING

A skilled manager of men is not warlike.
A skilled fighter is not angry.
One who is skilled at overcoming opposition
Does not become entangled with it.
One who is skilled at utilizing others
Behaves as their inferior.

Those principles are referred to as
The Virtue of not contending,
Making use of the strengths of others,
And *matching heaven.*
They are the highest achievements
Of the ancients.

69.
CAUTION

Accomplished fighters have a
saying:
"I dare not act the master,
But instead act the guest.
I dare not advance an inch,
But instead retreat a foot."

That is called
Pressing on without marching,
Seizing without arms,
Pushing without opposing,
Apprehending without weapons.

No calamity is greater
Than the results
Of thinking lightly of battle.
Thinking lightly of battle
Brings us closer to losing
What we value.

When opposing armies inflict
Violence on each other,
The side that would be
Sorrier to lose will prevail.

70.

MY WORDS

My words are very easy to know,
And very easy to put into practice.
But under heaven, no one can
Know them; no one can practice them.

Words have their ancestors;
Writers have their sovereigns.
But others without knowing these
Accordingly do not know me.

Those who know me are few in number;
Those who rule me are honored.
So, to resemble a wise man,
I put on coarse cloth and conceal
The jade.

71.

TO KNOW

To know *not-knowing*
Is the highest state.
To not know *knowing*
Is a defect.
Only those who know
That that defect
Is a defect
Are accordingly
Without it.

72.

THE WISE RULER

When the people do not respect
A figure of authority,
Then a greater figure of authority
Will appear—
One without a disdain for their
Dwellings
And without a loathing for their
Livelihoods.

Only a ruler who does not detest
Is accordingly not detested.

The wise ruler is self-knowing,
But not self-displaying.
He may love himself,
But he does not high-price himself.
He empties himself of the latter
And takes hold of the former.

73.

THE NET OF HEAVEN

Bravery acting through violence
Results in lives being destroyed.
Bravery acting through non-violence
Results in lives being saved.
The former of the two may give
Benefit, but may also give harm.
It is the one that heaven detests.
Who understands its reasons?
Even a wise man can be undecided,
And have difficulty with them.

Heaven's way:
It does not contend, yet it conquers.
It does not speak, yet it responds.
It does not call, yet all will come to it.
It is easygoing, yet it skillfully plans.

The net of heaven is *vast, vast.*
Its meshes are widely spaced,
But nothing escapes them.

74.

TAKING THE PLACE

The people do not fear death.
So what means could be used
To make death frighten them?
If they were made to constantly
Fear death,
Then anyone who acted in a
Manner acclaimed by the people
Could be seized and put to death.
Who then would dare to act
In a manner acclaimed by the people?

There is always One who presides
Over the elimination of life.
When someone takes the place of
That Executioner,
That is called *taking the place of*
The Great Blade-Wielder.
Those who have taken the place of
The Great Blade-Wielder
Rarely have not injured their hands.

75.

THOSE ABOVE

The people are increasingly suffering
From starvation
Because those above increasingly eat
Excessive quantities of their grain
As tax.
So the people starve.

The people are increasingly difficult
To govern
Because those above increasingly act
As if they possess them.
So the people resist authority.

The people increasingly think lightly
Of death
Because those above increasingly ask
That they grow more generous.
So the people take death lightly.

Only those without the use of life
Act as if to take death lightly
Is better than to value living.

76.

THE DISCIPLES

At a man's birth,
He is pliant and tender.
At his death,
He is hard and unyielding.
The ten thousand things—
The grass, the trees—
In life are supple and delicate,
In death are dry and decayed.
So the hard and unyielding
Are disciples of death;
The pliant and tender
Are disciples of life.

That is why an inflexible army
As a rule will not win,
And why an inflexible tree
Will be made into lumber.

The unyielding mighty
Shall be brought down.
The pliant and tender
Shall be elevated.

77.

HEAVEN'S WAY
THE WISE II

Heaven's way is like the act of
Drawing a bow,
In which the top end is lowered
And the bottom end is raised,
The height is decreased, and the
Shallow space between the string
And the bow is made full.

Heaven's way is to take away from
The excessive
And add on to the insufficient.
Man's way as a rule, however, is
Not like that—
He takes from those who do not have
Enough
In order to give to those who have
An excess.
Who is able to have an abundance
To offer to the world?
One who only has The Way.

The wise act, but do not rely on
Action.
They achieve merit, but do not
Reside in it.
They have no desire to appear
Worthy of acclaim.

78.

THE SOFT AND THE HARD
RESPONSIBILITY

Under heaven, nothing is softer
And weaker than water.
Yet for attacking the hard and strong,
Nothing is capable of excelling it—
There is nothing that can take its place.

The weak wins over the strong,
The soft wins over the hard.
Under heaven, no one does not know that;
But no one is capable of applying it.

A wise man has said:
"One who can shoulder responsibility
For the dirt and dishonor of the state
Can be called Lord of the Land.
One who can shoulder responsibility
For the ill fortune of the nation
Can be called All-Under-Heaven's Ruler,"

Proper words can seem contrary.

79.

OBLIGATIONS

An agreement entered into
With great resentment
Must contain an excess of ill will.
How can this be considered
As being good?
Rightly and accordingly,
The wise man holds
The left contract-slip
Listing his obligations,
And does not dispute with
The other party.

Those with Virtue
Manage their agreements.
Those without Virtue
Manage the collection of tax.

The Way of Heaven is without
Obligations to relatives—
So it consistently gives to
The good.

80.

Deleted—see the notes on this chapter

81.

SINCERE WORDS
THE WISE III
THE WAY OF THE WISE

Sincere words are not *sweet;*
Sweet words are not *sincere.*
The good are not *argumentative;*
The argumentative are not *good.*
The knowing are not of *"wide knowledge";*
Those of "wide knowledge" are not *knowing.*

The wise do not *accumulate—*
Expending all in doing for others,
They then have more.
Expending all in giving to others,
They then have much more.

The Way of Heaven is sharp,
But does not injure.
The way of the wise acts,
But does not contend.

CHAPTER NOTES:
WALKING THE MAZE

IN WRITING THE CHAPTER NOTES THAT FOLLOW, I chose not to explain every character-definition choice I made or mention every instance in which an ancient-character meaning was employed, but to instead cover only those choices that differed most significantly from the usual. Some chapters seemed to require more explanations than others—Chapter One, for example, of which the most lengthy analysis I've read occupies more than twenty pages of a book on the *Tao Te Ching*. And though I prefer the "less is more" approach to writing, some things did need to be said.

1.

THE WAY

"Lao-tzŭs philosophy is all here. The remaining five thousand words only expand on this first verse [chapter]." So wrote the Ming Dynasty Ch'an (Zen) Buddhist writer Te-ch'ing, translated here by Red Pine from his *Lao-tzu's Taoteching*. A problem lurking behind Te-ch'ing's very perceptive assessment is: Those who don't understand what is said in Chapter One won't understand a good deal of what is said in many chapters beyond it.

In the text of my first stanza the author is, I believe, introducing the distinctions he elaborates on in his next statements and in other chapters—rather than, as tradition has it, claiming that The Eternal Way, *which he tells about in this chapter and elsewhere*, cannot be told about.

"Origin" in the first line of my second stanza is from the text's *shih*, "beginning" or "origin," typically presented as "beginning." (Three exceptions: both Dr. Yi Wu and John C.H. Wu interpret *shih* in this chapter's context as "origin"; James Legge interprets it as "Originator.") I favored "origin" because Chapter Twenty-Five, the "Genesis" of the *Tao Te Ching*, states that The Way was the predecessor or ancestor of heaven and earth (*hsien t'ien ti shêng*, "before heaven [and] earth birth"), rather than their beginning.

"Without-Name" (*wu ming*) in the second stanza is The Way of Heaven (*t'ien tao*)—heavenly spirit, its true name unknown. "Has-Name" (*yu ming*) is The Valley Spirit (*ku shên*). "The Mother of Every Earthly Being" is literally "ten thousand things' mother" (*wan wu chih mu*).

"Without-Form" (*wu*, literally "non-being") in the third stanza is the invisible Way of Heaven. "Has-Form" (*yu*, literally "being") is the visible-in-its-manifestations Valley Spirit.

Also regarding the third stanza: My interpretation of *ch'ang wu yü*, the first three characters of the first statement, and that of *ch'ang yu yü*, the first three characters of the second statement, differ from all I've seen, except for that by Dr. Yi Wu. To define the terms in question:

Ch'ang, depending on context, can mean "constant, unchanging, consistent" or "eternal, everlasting." *Wu* can mean "without, absence of," "non-being, non-existence," or "emptiness, nothingness." *Yu* can mean "have, possess" or "being, existence." *Yü* means "desire, wish, long for."

Other interpreters interpret *ch'ang wu yü* in the context of this chapter as meaning "constantly [or "consistently"] without desire," and interpret *ch'ang yu yü* as meaning "constantly [or "consistently"] having desire," which produces interpretations such as:

Constantly without desire, one can observe its mysteries.
Constantly with desire, one can observe its manifestations.

But in such an interpretation, to which power designated in the first two stanzas does each "its" (*ch'i*) refer? Another point: Such an interpretation breaks the pattern of the two previous stanzas' texts—the pattern of differentiating between a *this* Way and a *that* Way. A third point: Such an interpretation bends (or breaks) the meaning of each statement's fourth character, *i* ("yee")—which in this context means "in order to"—to make the beginning of each statement link up with the characters that follow it. In other words, that sort of beginning doesn't work.

Taking my cue from those problems, I interpreted *ch'ang wu yü* in this case as meaning "consistently *Non-Being* desire" (in standard English, "consistently desire Non-Being") and interpreted *ch'ang yu yü* as meaning "consistently *Being* desire" (in standard English, "consistently desire Being"), thereby producing a pair of directive statements:

Consistently desire Non-Being in order to study its [Non-Being's] mysteries.
Consistently desire Being in order to study its [Being's] frontiers.

Which, as far as I could see, solved all the problems. Incidentally, "frontiers" at the end of the second statement is the definition of the character *chiao*, even though nobody else seems to use the word there.

Finally, for clarity and for consistency with the second stanza's terms, I replaced "Non-Being" with "Without-Form" and replaced "Being" with "Has-Form":

Consistently desire Without-Form in order to study its mysteries.
Consistently desire Has-Form in order to study its frontiers.

In my final stanza's first line, "the previous two" is my in-that-context interpretation of *tz'ŭ* (now meaning "this" or "these") *liang* ("two"). The ancient meaning of *tz'ŭ* was "to turn on one's heel[s]"—here signifying, I believe, *what one sees by looking back,* or *the previous.* "These," its brush-character definition, used in all other English-language editions I've seen, is a *chia-chieh,* a "false/borrowed" meaning.

Also in that first line, "same energy" is from *t'ung* ("fit together, join," "conform," "alike, identical, same") *ch'u* ("come forth," "go out," "proceed from," "appear," "produce, issue, beget"). Those dictionary definitions of *ch'u* didn't seem to fit the context, so I looked up *ch'u*'s ancient ancestor and found that the pictographic character had evolved from curved lines depicting an unfolding blossom (or, said some sources, growing leaves) to straight lines depicting plant stalks growing up out of the ground. Those images in the chapter's context suggested that the character might originally have also had a more basic meaning: energy—*that which* produces, issues, etc. Or did the author simply use it to *mean* that? Following "energy" to see where it would lead, I interpreted *t'ung ch'u* as "[are the] same energy." Which, when I considered the rest of the stanza and what had preceded it, seemed to fit. The traditional interpretation of *t'ung ch'u* in this chapter is "emerge together" ("together emerge") or "come from the same source," referring to the traditional interpretation's "mysteries" and "manifestations," rather than to their originators.

"Growing" and "increasing" in my final stanza's fourth and fifth lines are from *chih*, which at first meant "grow, develop," "continue, progress," but which somewhat later, still in ancient times—as can be deduced from its variety of relevant usages in the *Tao Te Ching*—came to also mean what it exclusively means now: "he," "she," "it," "them," or a sign of the possessive. In three other places in the chapter's text, *chih* is used as a possessive.

In the text of my first three stanzas, as I understand it, the author distinguishes between what he in later chapters refers to as The Way of Heaven and The Valley Spirit. Then, in the text of my final stanza, he tells us that their different designations (*i ming*, "different names/titles/designations")—those distinguishing between the earthly and the ethereal, the visible and the invisible—are describing two distinct aspects of the one creative energy. Putting the distinctions together, he forms *chih hsüan*, "growing darkness"—a fine touch, like that of a great magician.

The above *hsüan*, one of the most important characters and concepts in Taoism, means "dark," "deep," "profound," "mystical," "mysterious." It could be considered the ultimate *yin*. Another *yin* character is in the text of my third and fourth stanzas: *miao*, which I interpreted in context as "mysteries." Its very feminine definitions are "thin," "delicate," "young," "fine," "beautiful," "subtle," "wonderful," "mysterious."

On the subject of *mysterious*: All but one of the many interpretations I've read of this chapter make what the author says within it seem mystifying, and make chapters after it seem confusing, because those interpretations are apparently based on the belief that he is telling about one Way, "the eternal Way" (which they confusingly have him say cannot be told about), when he's actually telling about *two aspects of* the one Way—The Way of Heaven ("Without-Name," "Non-Being") and The Valley Spirit ("Has-Name," "Being")—both of which play their parts in the chapters that follow. If one looks at *tao k'o tao*, "way can be wayed," as "way can be followed" rather than as "way can be told," carefully considers the meanings-choices of all the characters, applying their ancient meanings whenever these differ from those of their descendants, and also takes into consideration what the author says in other chapters—rather than being intimidated by historic precedent into conformity with the traditional (Confucian scholar) interpretation—the structure and simplicity of what the chapter is saying can be seen:

> way can be wayed *not* eternal way
> name can be named *not* eternal name
> without name heaven earth 's origin

> has name 10,000 things 's mother
> so consistently non-being desire in order to
>   view/inspect its mysteries
> consistently being desire in order to
>   view/inspect its frontiers
> previous two : same energy but different
>   designations
> joined called growing darkness
> darkness growing again/yet again darkness
> many mysteries 's gateway

For my commentary on Wang Pi's interpretation of *tao k'o tao*, "way can be wayed," as "way can be told," see my notes on Chapter Thirty-Five.

2.
OPPOSITES
THE WISE

Chapter Two, like some other chapters of the *Way Virtue Classic*, concerns what seem to be two separate subjects. So I split it into two sections.

The first section has to do with the relationship of opposites, which create, clarify, conquer, and counterbalance each other in a dance of mutual dependency, like that of *yin* and *yang*, The Dark and The Light.

The text of my first section's first stanza has been interpreted in various ways. My character-by-character translation, using original meanings, is:

> heaven under all know goodness it acts goodness then
>   evil declines
> all know harmony it acts harmony then not harmony
>   declines

The first above-translated statement's fifth-and-eighth character, *mei* (originally made up of "sheep" plus "man"), meant "gentle," "peaceful," "good," or "sweet"—a "gentle man" or "like a gentle man." Its brush-written descendant ("sheep" plus "great") means "beautiful" or "excellent"—meanings used throughout other interpretations of the *Tao Te Ching*, which present it in this chapter as "beauty." The statement's next-to-last character, *o* (often mistakenly given as *wu*), is made up of "deformed" or "ugly" plus "heart"—a "deformed or ugly heart"—and means "evil, wicked." Other interpretations present it in this chapter as "ugliness" (leaving out "heart"), to serve as the opposite of "beauty."

The second statement's third-and-sixth character, *shan*, is made up of "sheep" (signifying *peace)* above "dispute," and pictographically means "harmony/peace/good feelings restored after a quarrel." By extension, it means "good," "virtuous," "kind," "honest"—and from "good," by extension, "clever" or "skillful." Other interpretations present *shan* here as "goodness."

Following the statements that I made into the second stanza were two that I translated/interpreted as: "Sound and voice harmonize with each other; front and back follow each other." They didn't fit into the theme of *opposite characteristics*—they seemed to have been added by someone who didn't grasp the *interplay of opposites* idea. So I eliminated them.

The second section concerns the behavior of the wise and the ten thousand things whose actions they emulate. My interpretation of the text differs greatly from all others I've seen. To be specific:

Lines one through four, unusual—or possibly unique—though their wording may seem, are as close to literal translations as I could manage.

"Why?" following line four is my in-context interpretation of *yen*, which is used to mean "why?" "how?" or "where?" It can also be used as a final particle. In the text, it followed the characters of my line six, coming after *tso*, "act," "do," "arise," "appear": "Ten thousand things act why? but not speak." *Yen* as a final particle made no sense in this case. As a question, it appeared to be in the wrong place. (Other interpretations, I've noticed, leave it out.) Assuming that it was meant as a question, I moved it to precede the above sentence, where it seemed to belong.

I read the text of line seven onward as clearly referring to the ten thousand things, rather than to the wise as most other interpreters have done. They modify the wording to shift focus back to the "wise man" or "wise men" mentioned in the beginning, producing statements such as "The ten thousand things arise, but the sage pays no attention to them"—very uncharacteristic of the ten-thousand-things-observing author, but nearly identical to a passage in a story by Taoism's second-most-quoted writer, Chuang-tzŭ.

In line eleven, "only they" is from the text's *fu* ("man," "men," or "the one or ones in question") *wei* ("only"). (In Chinese, *wei*, "only," typically follows rather than precedes whatever it's referring to.) "Men" made no sense in context—"Only men do not reside in their achievements"—so that left "the ones in question," which to me, according to what precedes *fu wei* in the text (*wan wu tso erh pu tz'u*, "ten thousand things act but not speak"), refers to the ten thousand things.

The last four lines are my interpretation of the text's *fu wei fu chü shih i pu ch'ü,* "The ones in question only not dwell therefore not empty/vacate/leave." "Not dwell therefore not leave" seemed ridiculously obvious—if you don't dwell in something, you obviously don't leave it. After wondering for days about what the author could have meant, I concluded that the most likely solution to the puzzle was that there was something missing just before the last character, *ch'ü*. I decided on a character such as *yu*, "melancholy, sad, sorry," "anxious," which produced: "Only they [do] not dwell [in their achievements, and are] therefore not sorry to leave [them]." The usual interpretation goes something like: "Because the sage does not dwell on his achievements, they therefore do not leave him." Aside from what I pointed out in the two previous paragraphs, which indicate that the ten thousand things, not the wise man/men, are the subject of the sentence, *ch'ü* means "dwell in, reside in, live in, exist in, inhabit, occupy" or "stop in, rest in"—not "dwell on." I interpreted *chü* as "lingering" (from "stop in, rest in") in line ten and as "reside in" (from "dwell in, reside in, live in, exist in, inhabit, occupy") in line eleven.

In line one, I interpreted *ch'u*—another character meaning "dwell in," etc.—as "exist in."

Finally: In various chapters, the author uses *chü* or *ch'u* ("dwell in," etc.) to indicate a mental or emotional attachment, rather than a physical state.

3.
NO DESIRE, NO CONTENTION

Some of the "wise government" chapters of the *Tao Te Ching* can be easily misunderstood—and have been, I now believe, even by later Taoist writers. This one is interpreted in all other editions I've seen as claiming that a wise government *"empties the people's minds and fills their bellies."* It *"weakens their ambitions and strengthens their bones"*—which *"causes the people to exist without knowledge. . . . It causes the knowledgeable to not dare to take* [rebellious] *action."* After analyzing the characters, I concluded that the author is instead saying that wise governing makes the people contented with what they have and with who and what they are, rather than contending with others for what they have been told they ought to want and for who and what they have been told they ought to be—contention that fragments their society and wastes their energy on attempts to fulfill externally created desires.

Regarding *"empties the people's minds"*: "Hearts and minds" in my first two stanzas is from *hsin*, which can mean "heart," "mind," or both. In line four of my second stanza, to clarify what I believe in context is being said (see the preceding stanza's statements), I added "of that discontent."

Regarding *"weakens their ambitions"*: *Chih*, long presented as "ambition," means "will, resolution, a purpose that is *fixed* [my emphasis]." I interpreted it in this chapter's context as "obstinacy" (second stanza, line six).

Regarding *"causes the people to exist without knowledge. . . . It causes the knowledgeable to not dare to take action"*: The character presented in other interpretations as "knowledge" is *chih* (a different character from the *chih* above), the definition of which is "knowing"—meaning either "possessing knowledge," "perceptive," "wise," or "understanding," depending on context (or, when speaking, on intonation—middle-rising tone, high-falling tone, etc.). But does feeding people prevent them from *possessing knowledge*? How could it do such a thing? As China's history—or any other nation's history—shows, well-fed people are far more eager to gain and use knowledge than are the *not*-well-fed. And in China, it's been poor, hungry peasants, anger-driven agitators, and greedy, over-ambitious princes—not the *intelligentsia*—who have started rebellions. So what does the author mean in this case by *chih*?

From antiquity, *chih* has consisted of an arrow alongside a mouth, meaning "arrow-mouth." *Chih*'s literal translations are "fast mouth," "fast talker," or "quick opinion"—signifying, say the dictionaries, *someone who quickly tells the answer to a question or the solution to a problem*. Wondering what the author could mean by *chih* in this context, and considering that he sometimes seems to use the most basic "picture" meanings of characters—which were likely among the original definitions—I concluded that "fast talk" and "fast talkers" would fit the situation (second stanza, lines nine and eleven). "Fast talkers" in this chapter's context would mean *agitators*.

In my last stanza, I added "manage without forcing" (line two) for clarity of meaning. The phrase before that, "do without doing," is a literal translation of the text's *wei wu wei*. That term and its cousin, *wu wei*, are frequently used in the *Tao Te Ching*. To explain in what way, and why:

The character *wei* depicts a female monkey with clawing hands. According to my research, the ancient Chinese regarded the female monkey as the animal most inclined to overhandle whatever it is holding or using. Despite *wei*'s definitions as "do," "act," "cause," "make," "practice," or "manage," the author often uses the character according to its "picture" to mean *overdo*—to fuss with or force. In the *Tao Te Ching*, *wei wu wei* tends to mean *do without fussing, forcing, or straining*. According to the author, as various "political" chapters show, the wise ruler or wise government works with the people and does not "monkey" with, injure, or oppress them.

4.
DEEP WATER

My interpretation of this chapter differs radically from all others I've seen. It's based on the characters of the standard text—with one exception, explained below—but interprets some of them differently from the long-standing tradition. Regarding that exceptional character:

My first stanza begins with the following sentence: "The Way swirls round and round like a whirlpool, and at its center it may seem to not be full." The characters of the sentence's text are *tao ch'ung erh yung chih huo pu ying*, classical (brush-character) definitions of which are:

way surge/heave/be agitated/rush against and/yet/but to use/
employ he/she/it unknown/uncertain/perhaps not full

The usual rendering of that sentence goes something like: "The Way is like an empty bowl that can be used, but is [redundantly?] never full."

When I read the definitions-list I'd compiled of that opening sentence, I received the impression that the characters were saying something completely unlike the various interpretations I'd seen. But I couldn't determine what that something was because I was puzzled by the fourth character, *yung*, the definitions of which in context made no sense to me. So I did some research.

The ancient ancestor of *yung*, I learned, depicted the bronze tripod used to support offertory vessels employed in temple services. It meant (as it does still) "to use, employ."

Next to the ancestor of *yung* in an analysis of similar characters was, I noticed, the nearly identical ancestor of the character *chung*. The ancient ancestor of *chung*–as in *chung kuo*, "Center Nation," the Chinese name for China–depicted a traditional Chinese target, pierced in its center by an arrow represented by a vertical line. The character meant "center," "to hit the center," "at the center," and so on. The writing-brush scribes later simplified the target's outline to a square, making the two characters easy to distinguish from each other. But their ancestors differ from each other only in two small ways: In *yung*, "to use," the two horizontal lines depicting the crossbars of the tripod–which are the same distance apart as are the two horizontal lines depicting the target's top and bottom in *chung*–are placed slightly lower on the verticals; and above them, projecting to the right from the middle vertical, is a short, horizontal line (to distinguish the character from *chung*?).

When I considered how difficult it is at a glance to differentiate the ancestor of *chung* from that of *yung*–so difficult that one analytical dictionary failed to do so–I wondered if a copyist long ago could have read the former as the latter. I replaced *yung* in the text with *chung*, and the result made sense. And from that, my interpretation was born.

In this chapter, The Way is described by three characters, each containing *shui*, "water":

The first one, ch'ung–represented by "swirls round and round" in my first stanza, first line, and by my added second line, "like a whirlpool"–is made up of "water" plus "center" and as I've indicated above is defined (inadequately) in classical Chinese dictionaries as "surge," "heave," "be agitated," "rush against." A more literal translation would be "water rotating around a center." The usual interpretations of ch'ung in this chapter, as also indicated above, are "empty bowl," "empty vessel," and the like.

The second character used in this chapter to describe The Way, yüan, now meaning "abyss," "gulf"–represented in my first stanza's lines five and six as "dark water whirling at the bottom of an abyss"–now consists of the character for "water" plus a picture representing a whirlpool at the bottom of an abyss. The earlier of its two ancient forms consisted of a picture of water in a circle, meaning "whirlpool." Somewhat later, its water–more economically depicted as un-circled but agitated–was placed between two cliffs, creating "whirlpool at the bottom of an abyss." The inclusion of the "water" character in the brush-written descendant is a redundancy, according to the dictionaries; but it gave me the idea for "dark"–which is what water at the bottom of an abyss would be. The typical interpretation of yüan in this chapter is "deep" or "fathomless." In the text, yüan is followed by an emphasis/exclamation character, so I italicized my interpretation of it.

The third descriptive character, chan–represented in my second stanza, first line, by "deep water"–is formed by "water" plus "very," "much." Its most relevant classical dictionary definitions are "to sink in water," "to soak," "tranquil, serene." But from chan's components and the context, I concluded that one of its original meanings must have been "deep water." The usual interpretation in this chapter is "deep." Chan is followed in the text by an emphasis/exclamation character, so I italicized my interpretation of it.

In my second stanza's last line, "Supreme Ruler" is from the text's ti (not to be confused with ti, "earth"), explained by Robert Hendricks in his Te-Tao Ching (The Modern Library, New York, 1993):

> "Lord" (Ti) was the name of the supreme deity of the Shang people (traditional dates 1766-1122 BCE); Ti was also used as a name for the supreme god of the Chou (1122-221 BCE), though they more commonly used the name "Heaven" (T'ien).

One of the intriguing things about Chapter Four is its statement that The Way, "The Ancestor of the Ten Thousand Things," existed before any "Lord" or "Supreme Ruler." In Chapter Thirty-Four, the author describes how different the behavior of "The Great Way" is from that of a lord of any kind, capitalized or not–operating as it does through modesty, generosity, compassion, and flexibility, maintaining by its use of them a mysterious power that nothing can resist. It rules not from the top down (*yang*) but from the bottom up (*yin*).

Following the text of my first stanza were four statements, character-for-character identical to four in Chapter Fifty-Six: "Break off the pointed. Untangle the disordered. Harmonize with the light. Join with the dust." Most of the interpretations I've seen of this chapter modify the statements to fit in the chapter's context by preceding each one with "it": "It breaks off the pointed," and so on. I finally decided that, modified or not, the statements simply didn't fit—they abruptly interrupted the *water* theme with images unrelated to the rest. So I eliminated them.

5.
DELETED

No commentary on or explanation of what is traditionally considered the fifth chapter has ever been able to convince me that its writing is the work of the author of the *Tao Te Ching*. The alleged chapter reflects the Machiavellian attitude of the Legalist school of philosophy, which had originated before the Warring States period. But that doesn't necessarily mean that it's the work of a Legalist writer; it could just as well be the work of an old sourpuss.

The first part of the alleged chapter claims that heaven and earth have no *jên* ("benevolence," "kindness," "humanity")—that they treat the ten thousand things as "straw dogs," handmade animals used to take the place of real animals in a sacrifice, then cast aside. It also claims that the wise man has no *jên* either—that he treats *the people* as straw dogs. Both statements contradict those made throughout the *Way Virtue Classic*.

Although the *Tao Te Ching*'s author belittles *jên*, "benevolence," as a codified Confucian principle in Chapter Eighteen, he praises *jên* in its higher, more natural manifestations in Chapter Thirty-Eight. And in chapter after chapter he writes of the benevolent nature of heaven and earth, that of The Way of Heaven and The Valley Spirit, and recommends that the wise, the rulers, and everyone else emulate it. And he writes of the benevolent character and behavior of wise government.

The alleged chapter's second part, which is as odd and out-of-character as the first, compares the space between heaven and earth to a (Chinese) bellows. Nowhere else in the *Tao Te Ching* does the author concern himself with the space between heaven and earth. What relevance could it have to what he's writing about?

What is traditionally considered Chapter Five appears to me to be the work of someone who's trying to be smart, and who consequently does what people often do when they aspire to intelligence rather than possess it—make extreme statements.

6.

THE VALLEY SPIRIT

Those who take for their standard anything but Nature, the mistress of all masters, weary themselves in vain.

LEONARDO DA VINCI

"The spirit of the valley" [*ku shên*, "Valley Spirit"] has come to be a name for the activity of the Tao in all the realm of its [earthly] operation. "The female mystery" [*hsüan p'in*, "Mysterious Female"] is the Tao with a name of chapter 1, which is "the Mother of all things" [*wan wu chih mu*, "Ten Thousand Things' Mother"].

JAMES LEGGE

This chapter's short, simple-appearing, but deep description of The Valley Spirit—also known as The Mysterious Female—contains what could be the most important principle of the *Tao Te Ching*: Work with the laws of nature, the greatest power on Earth. Everything The Valley Spirit does, she does effortlessly. Work with her and life will be easier. Work against her and life will be difficult.

In the third and fourth lines of my first stanza, I changed "root of" to "connection between," as the use of *kên*, "root," "origin," or "source," in the text (*t'ien ti kên*, "heaven earth root") didn't make sense to me. The Way of Heaven, not The Valley Spirit, is the root, origin, or source of heaven and earth (Chapter Twenty-Five). The Valley Spirit is the connection between the two. I suspect that an early copyist misread a character, mistakenly substituted a sound-alike or look-alike character, confused The Valley Spirit with The Way of Heaven, or tried to "improve" things. I found that inconsistency in the use of characters is a good indicator of error or tampering.

(Some interesting possible originals of the chapter's contradictory *kên*, "root," "origin," "source," are: *kên*, "border, boundary"; *kuan*, "frontier-gate," "a pass," "connection"; *lao*, "silk or hempen thread," "connection." Other "connection" characters also contain the image of thread—which, if any such were the character used by the author, might have inspired the text of the second stanza.)

Mien mien jo ts'un, the characters that make up the text of the second stanza, translate in that order as: (1) "silk floss," "cotton wool," "soft, downy," "thin and long," "drawn out, continuous"; (2) the first character repeated; (3) "resemble, like," "as"; (4) "propagate," "survive, continue to exist." The character-sequence equivalent of English-language word order would be 3-1-2-4.

7.
ABLE TO ENDURE

Elsewhere in the *Way Virtue Classic*, we are told that heaven and The Way of Heaven are eternal (*ch'ang*). Here, however, in the text of my first stanza, we are told that heaven is merely *long* (*ch'ang*, "long"—a different character). We are also told here that *earth* is long—but with another "long" character, *ch'iu*. According to an analytical dictionary of classical Chinese characters, *ch'iu* means "a long *time*" (I'm adding the emphasis), while the ancient ancestor of this chapter's *ch'ang*, "long," was "used in matters pertaining to hair," and depicted hair so long that it must be tied and pinned. The character was later modified in meaning, says the dictionary, to indicate the long hair of manhood, after which the character's definition was extended to also mean "a long time or distance."

It seemed obvious to me that a copyist mistook one *ch'ang* for another. And it seemed to me that if the author had meant to say that both heaven's and earth's lives are merely *long*—which would have contradicted what he says in Chapter One onward—he would have used *ch'iu* to describe both. He is, to put it mildly, an economical writer. So I interpreted this chapter's *ch'ang* according to what I believe the author intended: *ch'ang*, "eternal."

A difficulty with the Chinese language, except for poets looking for rhymes, is that its sounds repeat, repeat, repeat. There are a great many characters and a much smaller number of character sounds. That's why intonation is used when speaking—to help differentiate between characters that otherwise would sound the same. For an example of this idiosyncrasy of the Chinese language, one classical Chinese dictionary lists twenty *ch'angs*, each of a different definition. The important thing for a copyist in a situation such as this chapter presents is to hear or look at *ch'ang*, *ming*, or whatever and not mistakenly write a sound-alike or look-alike character.

In the second stanza, I added "follows their example" (line one) and "he" (line two). I interpreted *shên*, "body" or "self" according to context, as "self" in line two and as "body" in lines four and five. "Self-interest" in lines seven and nine is from *ssŭ*, "personal," "selfish," "self-intertest."

8.
SUPERIOR GOODNESS

Regarding my first stanza, line four: The character *chêng* depicts two hands pulling a stick in opposite directions, and is defined as "to contend," "to wrangle." It is traditionally interpreted in various chapters of the *Tao Te Ching* as "compete." To me, the author means by it something more aggressive and less friendly than *compete*, so I used *contend* throughout this presentation.

In line five, I added "it flows to humble," to fill a gap in the text.

The text of my second stanza originally followed that of what is now my third stanza. It appeared to have been added as an afterthought. As such, it seemed to work better where I placed it. Its meaning was easy to be sure about, except for the last character, *yu*, generally presented in this chapter as "fault" or "blame":

men   only   not   contend   cause   no [literally "absence of"]   *yu*

In English-language word order:

Only men [who do] not contend cause no *yu*.

Yu is defined as "evils," "calamities," "transgressions," "errors," "fault," "blame." I decided that *evils* worked the best, especially considering the brutal contending of the Warring States period and its cause: *greed*. A critic of the resulting statement could say that, for example, those who passively go along with their government's warlike acts are not contending, yet they are causing evil; but in reality, while they may be supporting evil and enabling it to continue, they are not *causing* it.

The sketchy text of what is now my third stanza seems to have a near-infinite variety of mostly wordy interpretations. As an example of the text's structure, the characters of my first line are *chü shan ti*, "dwell/dwellings good earth/ground/land," which I interpreted as "Dwellings [that are] good [have] land," which I simplified to "Good dwellings have land."

The last word in line five, "healing," is from *chih*, "to cure," "to heal," "to govern." The typical English-language interpretation in this chapter is "maintain order" or an equivalent. To me, *healing* seemed more in line with what the author says about wise governing throughout the *Way Virtue Classic*.

In line six, "writings" is my most-likely unique interpretation of *shih*, dictionary-defined as "to serve," "affairs," "business," "office" (as in government office), or "matters." Other interpretations I've seen use those or similar meanings. However:

From ancient times, *shih* has consisted of the character for "he," "she," "they," or "it" above a pictograph of a hand holding the writing tube described in "Ancient Pictures, Ghostly Voices" and pictured on ancient bronze castings. The "picture" the character presents could signify *clerk* (business), *scribe* (office), or *writer* [affairs, matters), as well as what those people do (write) and deal with (writings). Going by what seemed to fit with the rest of the stanza's statements, I interpreted *shih* as "writings."

In the same line, "power" is from *nêng*, "ability," "talent," "strength," "power." The character, which depicts a bear, at first signified *strength*. It then became a slang term for *ability*, as a bear's great strength makes him very able. Other interpretations present this chapter's *nêng* as "ability." But "Good writings [or the usual interpretation-choices] have ability" seemed trite. In the other statements, the author reaches for more than the obvious. Also, the repeated character *shan* ("good," "kind," "virtuous," "clever," or "skill-ful") means more in this context than "skilled." Therefore: "Good writings have power."

Regarding the last line of the stanza: Traditionally in China, the timing of an action is considered as important as the action itself. An undertaking with the best plan and intentions behind it can come to nothing, or worse, if its timing is inappropriate.

9.
EXCESS

The rather stiff writing style of Chapter Nine's text made me suspect that it might not be the work of the *Tao Te Ching*'s author. But its theme and point of view seemed compatible with those stated elsewhere.

The chapter consists of four eight-character sentences and a final sentence of seven characters. The following is my character-by-character translation, which leaves out all probably irrelevant definitions for the sake of simplicity:

> hold and fill/overfill it not like it/that cease/excessive
> feel for/estimate and sharpen/thin it not able long protect
> gold jade fill hall not/not? it able to keep/to guard
> wealth honors and haughtiness self give they calamity
> good results succeed oneself retreat heaven 's way

The first sentence could be interpreted either as "To hold and fill [something] is not the same as overfilling it" or as "To hold and overfill [something] is not like stopping that." Most interpretations I've seen are variations on the latter of the two: "To fill a cup until it runs over is not as good as stopping short of the brim," or an equivalent. In either case, the point of that sentence, and the others, is: *Don't overdo it.*

In going over the text, I noticed that the character used for "no" or "not" in the third sentence was the negative or negative interrogative *mo*, rather than the usual *pu* used in the first two sentences. A negative interrogative as a possibility made no sense there, but it started me thinking: Maybe I could turn the first four sentences into thought-provoking questions, to bring the wording closer to the author's style elsewhere, as in Chapter Ten or (especially) Chapter Forty-Four. The rhyme scheme wrote itself.

10.
EMBRACING THE ONE

Chapter Ten concerns itself with meditation practices that had originated before the time of the *Tao Te Ching*.

Some scholars believe that the first character, *tsai*, which means "to carry," and which can be used as an exclamation/emphasis character, is actually the last character of Chapter Nine. As they point out, when it is removed the first question-asking statement matches the seven-character-plus-interrogative structure and rhythm of the others, and its wording makes a good deal more sense. I too believe that *tsai*, as an emphatic, belongs in Chapter Nine, as its inclusion there makes that text's seven-character last statement match the others in number. Its presence at the start of this chapter causes interpreters to redefine the should-be-first next character (*Ying*, "to regulate, manage") in order to try to make the sentence work.

P'o, which I Anglicize in line one as "earth-grounded spirit," is one of the two souls, or spirits, that Chinese folk religion believes the human being contains, the other one being the *hun*. The *p'o* is the "physical" soul that keeps everything in the body working properly. On the death of the body, the *p'o* disintegrates with it. The *hun* is the "spirit" soul that inhabits the body as a rider inhabits a carriage. When the body dies, the *hun* goes on to the spirit realm. (After religious Taoism formed, its doctrine-makers, who never seemed to pass up an opportunity to complicate things, declared that everyone has seven *p'o* and three *hun*. Very confusing.)

"The One" in line two is another term for The Way. In meditation, the practitioner "returns to The Source" or "embraces The One"—in each case, the concept is the same—blending with the source of all life as a raindrop blends with the sea, making no distinction between one and the other. After all, from the Taoist point of view, each *is* part of the other. Separation is an illusion. In meditation, one works to dissolve the illusion.

"Opening and closing the gates of heaven" (line four) refers to the practice of *ch'i* circulating, in this case during meditation. *Ch'i*, which I interpret in line six as "life force," is commonly defined as "vital energy." In *ch'i*-circulating practices, it emanates from the practitioner's palms like a subtle form of steam. The pictographic character *ch'i* depicts steam rising from rice. "The gates of heaven" in line four are the nostrils. Non-initiates refer to *ch'i*-circulating practices as "breathing exercises." (Before the *ch'i* meridians—energy channels—are opened, *ch'i* tends to be lazy and sluggish. Imagining the breath moving along the meridians "pulls" the *ch'i* through them. Eventually, once the meridians have been opened, *ch'i* can be sent to anywhere in the body by willing it there. Imagining it as breath speeds up the movement and exercises the *ch'i*.)

Regarding "like the female" (line five): The character the author uses is *tz'ŭ*, "female bird." The female bird—keeping still, her camouflage-like feathers blending with her nest while her brightly colored, vocal *yang* mate distracts predators—provides an appropriate *yin* image for deep meditation.

For what I considered better chronology, I moved the second question (lines four and five) from its original place later in the text.

The phrase that I worded as "cleaning the flaws from your deep [*hsüan*] vision [*lan*]" (line nine) is comparable to—and is the source of—"cleaning the inner mirror" in Zen. (*Zen* is the Japanese equivalent of the Chinese *Ch'an*, an individualistic form of Buddhism that was created by joining Taoist practices and attitudes to Buddhist doctrine.)

I eliminated the fourth sentence of the text, typically interpreted as "Loving the people and ruling the nation, can you be free of all knowing [or, as some interpreters erroneously have it, "cleverness"]?" (Another interpretation, using the pictographic meanings of *chih*, "knowing"—as I believe the author did in Chapter Three—would be: "Loving the people and ruling the nation, can you be free of all fast talking / speedy answers / quick opinions?") The sentence didn't fit the context of meditation and *ch'i* circulating.

Following the text of my interpretation were twenty characters. Sixteen of them were identical to those at the end of Chapter Fifty-One, and the other four were a shortened version of the six-character sentence preceding the sixteen. In Chapter Fifty-One, they fit the context; but in this one, they didn't. So I eliminated them.

11.
THE VALUE OF EMPTINESS

Chapter Eleven uses the hub of a wheel, the inside of a clay vessel, and the windows and doors of a house to illustrate in a down-to-earth manner the relationship between *yu*, "form," "existence," "being," and *wu*, "without form," "non-existence," "non-being." The following translation of the text of my third stanza can serve to show the author's use of characters:

> chisel   door[s]   window[s]   in order to   make   house
> in   its   non-existence   exist[s]   house   's   use[fulness]

In my first stanza, I added "in order to make a wheel" so the stanza's structure would match that of the next two stanzas (did someone leave out some characters?) and added the explanatory phrase "the hole in its hub."

In the next two stanzas, I added the explanatory phrases between the dashes.

In my final stanza, *li*, the last character in the text of the second line, translates as "sharp," "cutting," "clever," "profit," or "advantage." Other interpretations of this character in their great variety of final statements use one of the last two definitions, or an equivalent. To me, "profitable" and "advantageous" were too much like "useful"—from *yung*, the stanza's final character—to provide the necessary contrast with it. The material forms described in the previous stanzas, I considered, were made with *cleverness*. So "clever" is the definition I used.

My translation of the text of my final stanza was:

therefore   form   them   in order to   make   cleverness
without-form   them   in order to   make   usefulness

12.
MORE IS LESS

In Chinese tradition, the five colors are red, yellow, blue/green, white, and black. The five tones are C (*kung*), D (*shang*), E (*chiao*), G (*chih*), and A (*yü*). The five flavors are sweet, sour, bitter, acrid, and salty.

The text of my first stanza, translated, goes like this: "[The] five colors make people's eyes blind. [The] five tones make people's ears deaf. . . ." Or, more literally: "[The] five colors command/order people's eyes [to go] blind. . . ."

"Excessive racing and chasing" (first stanza, line seven) could be more fully stated as "excessive racing and chasing on horseback through the fields." (From the text's *ch'ih ch'eng t'ien lieh*, "fast/racing excess in-cultivated-field chase/hunt.") Such behavior would not have been practiced or approved of by the field workers.

In my second stanza, for clarity, I added "He attends to contentment and not to desire" (lines four and five).

In various chapters of the *Way Virtue Classic*, including this one, the author warns of the negative emotional, spiritual, and societal effects of conspicuous consumption, consumer lifestyle, and fast living long before those terms would come into existence. In this chapter, he appears to be criticizing the overindulgence, extravagant buying habits, and frivolous pursuits of the wealthy class or the nobility—his *milieu*, so later chapters indicate, but one that he would seem to not feel comfortable in. Since I myself have never felt comfortable in such an environment, he has my complete sympathy.

13.
ENTRUSTED WITH THE WORLD

There are probably as many interpretations of Chapter Thirteen as there are interpreters of the *Way Virtue Classic*. It would seem that its statements are so cryptically simple that no two interpreters can agree on their meanings.

The following is my translation sketch of the nine-character text of the first stanza. Some of the definitions are rearranged here from their dictionary-given sequences in order to more simply show how I arrived at my interpretation:

> *ch'ung* (favor, grace, kindness) *ju* (disgrace, to reveal disgrace, dishonor, insult, defile, humble, shame) *jo* (if, to be as, as if, to resemble, to follow, to be in sympathy with) *ch'ing* (fear, fright, alarm) *kuei* (honor, value) *ta* (great) *huan* (affliction, sorrow) *jo* (if, to be as, as if, to resemble, to follow, to be in sympathy with) *shên* (the self, the body, personal, the whole life)

Rather than try to make some of the definitions make sense in context, I just looked at all of them, pretending that I'd never seen them before and that I'd never read even one interpretation of the chapter. After a while, one definition of each character seemed to stand out from the rest–the first one listed above for each character–producing the statements "Favor, disgrace if fear. Honor, great affliction if self." Which I immediately understood. After that, the rest of the text was fairly easy to interpret.

The following is my translation of the text of my final stanza:

> consequently   value   use [of]   self   to act [for]   heaven   under
>   to be as   able   to lodge at   heaven   under
> love [to]   use   self   to act [for]   heaven   under   to be as   able
>   to [be] entrust[ed] with   heaven   under

My interpretation of that translation was originally my fourth stanza, the final one of the chapter. But I thought that its text's first character–*ku*, "consequently," "therefore," "so"–didn't make an adequately clear transition from what had preceded it to the concluding characters. So I replaced the "consequently" with what became my fourth stanza.

14.
THE WAY OF HEAVEN

In this chapter, the author defines the indefinable Way of Heaven by saying what it's *not*. Then at the end–at least in my interpretation–he tells how one can know it: by knowing its ancient beginning (which he describes in Chapter Twenty-Five).

There are three very strange characters in this chapter–*i, hsi,* and *huang*–all of which are likely mistakes. But the intended meanings in the first two cases can be deduced from their surroundings:

In my first stanza, "invisible" (line two) and "inaudible" (line four) are my substitutes for, respectively, *i* ("foreigner, barbarian," "destroy, kill," "raze to the ground, level," "to feel at ease, tranquil," "of the same sort," "ordinary, vulgar ") and *hsi* ("few, rare," "seldom," "to hope"). Some other interpreters have done their best to explain the presence of those ridiculously out-of-place characters, but I couldn't do the same. Interpreting the author's intended meanings by context, it seemed obvious to me that if something cannot be seen (line one), it is therefore *invisible* (or formless), and that if something cannot be heard (line three), it is therefore *inaudible* (or silent).

"Intangible" (line six) is my in-context ("cannot be grasped") version of *wei*, "small, minute, trifling," "hidden," "to fade, diminish."

"The One" in the final line of my first stanza is from another *i*, "one"–"The One" being another term for The Way.

In my second stanza, line five, "stretches, stretches" is my interpretation of the text's *shêng shêng*, "cord, cord" or "string, string." As was done in Chapter Six, thread, cord, or string has long been used in Chinese writing as a symbol of continuity or infinity.

The Chinese text of the two statements that now occupy lines three and four of my second stanza followed the text of my third stanza. I moved them to where they seemed to better fit.

The final character in the text of my third stanza–*huang*, "agitated, flustered," "wild," "mad"–made no sense whatsoever. Looking through the analytical dictionaries, I found a sound-alike, closely related *huang*, "uncertain," which seemed a likely original. The latter *huang*, "uncertain," differs from the former by its inclusion of the character for "sun." (Did a copyist leave out the sun, making the character agitated, flustered, wild, and mad?)

In the final line of my final stanza, "clarifying" is my interpretation of *chi*, "unravel threads," "sort out, arrange," "regulate, make law," "narrate," "record."

The text of the chapter's last two lines–which I translated as "Able know ancient beginning this called Way unravel/sort out"–seems to be interpreted differently by everyone.

15.
THE ANCIENT MASTERS
PATIENCE

I ended up making a separate section of what started out as my third stanza because it seemed a separate piece of writing–inspired though it may have been by the final characters of what I made into my second stanza.

The text of that second stanza has an emphasis/exclamation character after the first character of each description–except for the initial one, which is followed (mistakenly, I believe) by an interrogative character instead–so I italicized each introductory word for emphasis.

Also in the second stanza, "break up" (line seven) is my interpretation of *shih*, "loosen," "set free," interpreted in other editions as "melt."

Regarding the second section's last three lines: It seems that everyone who chooses from the possible definitions of the characters in the text comes up with an interpretation different from those of the other interpreters. My character-by-character translation, with two words added—the first because there seemed to be a character missing after *nêng*, "able," "can"—is:

> who? can [produce] peace by means of long time moving/
> exciting/rousing it [to] gradually grow

The text has more characters following those of the above question. I translated/ interpreted them, as literally as possible, as: "Those who protect The Ancient Way [or "the former way"] do not want excess. Only those who are not excessive are therefore able to wear out [the character *pi*, "worn out," "shabby," "poor", "miserable, "vile", depicts torn cloth] and not newly achieve." I eliminated all that because it appeared to be something added to the text (or copied by a drunken copyist?), because it didn't seem to fit, and because I just plain didn't understand it—nor do I understand any of the very loose English-language interpretations of it that I've seen. For those reasons, I didn't feel right about passing it along as part of the *Tao Te Ching*.

16.
RETURNING TO THE SOURCE

The Taoist phrase *kuei kên*, "return to The Source," can mean to die and return to The Way of Heaven, or it can mean to renew contact with it while alive, as in meditation.

In the first stanza, the former of the two above meanings applies. The many non-human forms of life visualized by the author don't separate themselves from The Source, so they don't need to "return to" it in life.

In the other stanzas, the phrase's second meaning seems intended. The author, having in his meditative practice envisioned various forms of life returning to The Source, describes what meditators can achieve through habitual mental and emotional reacquaintance with it.

In the first stanza, I added "On my" (line one) and "in my mind" (line five). To me, they or their equivalents were at least implied in the text, if they were not originally present—considering that the statement following the text of my first sentence starts with *wu*, "I." The author appears to be writing about his own practice rather than, as other interpretations present the material, telling others how to meditate.

"Submersion of the self," the next-to-last line of the third stanza, commonly interpreted as "death of the body" or something similar, is my interpretation of *mo* ("to submerge, to sink in water," or, by extension, "to disappear") *shên* ("the self" or "the body," depending on context). *Mo*, "submerge," consists of *shui*, "water," plus *mu*, "to dive." (Instead of *mo*, some printings of the standard text mistakenly have the similar character *mu*—not the same as *mu*, "to dive"—which means "to die, to perish.") *Submerging the self*—the self as an entity separate from The Way and its creations—is what Taoist meditation is about.

Why is submerging the self important? Those who recognize that they are not separate from the world of nature or from other human beings do not clear-cut Earth's forests out of existence, poison its water, destroy its animal life, kill other people, steal others' possessions, or rob the poor in order to feed the wealthy. They instead find more constructive and appreciative ways to use their energies, abilities, and time.

17.
THE FINEST RULER

The main theme of this chapter is that the finest ruler (*t'ai shang*, "supreme highest") governs so effectively using the principle of *wu wei* (without forcing or fussing with) that the people he rules (*hsia*, "[those] below") are hardly aware of him. When something goes well, the people believe that they themselves accomplished it. In other words, the best ruler is *yin*—modest, unpretentious, with respect for, and with faith in, those he rules.

The last four lines of my first stanza are my interpretation of the text's *hsin pu tsu yen yu pu hsin yen*, "Faith not sufficient why?/emphasis. Has/have not faith why?/ emphasis." The repeated character *yen* can mean "why?" or "how?" or can be used, as it apparently is here, to add weight to the end of a statement. The characters, which seem to be missing some helpers, form the sort of puzzle that the *Way Virtue Classic* is infamous for. I checked twelve English-language *Tao Te Ching*s and found that each one had a different interpretation of the characters. I chose what seemed the most likely translation: "[His] faith [in them is] *not sufficient*. [So they] *have not faith* [in him]." Which became: "He has insufficient faith in *them*, so they have no faith in *him*."

In the first two lines of my second stanza, "thoughtful, far-seeing, and foreseeing" is from *yu*, "think," "foreseeing," "far-reaching." I added "A great ruler is" to the beginning of the statement (did someone leave out a couple of characters?), as otherwise it would have seemed to be referring to the lowest ruler, despised by his people, at the end of the previous stanza.

In the second and third lines, I added "and so keeps them to himself" to clarify what I believe is being said—that the finest ruler doesn't boast about his achievements, thereby allowing his people to take credit.

18.
A GREAT FALSEHOOD

The Great Way has been abandoned—
We have Benevolence[1] and Righteousness.[2]
Clever Knowing[3] has arisen—
We have a great falsehood.
Family Relations[4] have lost their harmony—
We have Filial Piety[5] and Maternal Affection.[6]
The nation's household is in darkness
And disorder—
We have Loyal Ministers.[7]

In the declining years of the Chou Dynasty, Confucianism appeared, with its codified, guiding principles of (listed here in the order given above): (1) *jên* (benevolence, kindness, humanity); (2) *i* (righteousness); (3) *chih* (knowing, perception, wisdom); (4) *liu ch'in* (the "six relationships," which codified proper status and behavior within families; (5) *hsiao* (filial piety); (6) *tz'ŭ* (maternal affection, compassion); (7) *chung* (loyalty); also *hsin* (sincerity), *li* (propriety, rites, sacrifices), and *shu* (reciprocity—which, as Confucianism's founder stated, meant "Do not do to others what you would not have them do to you").

Confucianism had been founded by a man focused on the great rulers of the past, as well as on creating strict order with which to eliminate the chaos of the age. In the Han Dynasty (206 BCE–220 CE), when it became the national religion, Confucianism locked the empire into a system of reverence for a frozen-in-time, theme park-like re-creation of ancient Chinese history—a constrictive system of governmental and social rules, protocol, and hierarchies that determined all relationships and turned individuals into cogs in Confucian governmental/societal wheels. Confucianism's founder, K'ung Fu-tzŭ, had managed to overlook a vital reality: The great men of the past had been great not because they had looked back but because they had looked forward.

(Although the historian Ssu-ma Ch'ien's "biography" of "Master Lao" is in my opinion historical fiction, it does include a telling remark that the Master Lao of the legend makes to Master K'ung: "The men you talk about are dead, and their bones have crumbled to dust—only their words remain.")

After the collapse of the Han Dynasty, China's straitjacketing Confucian rule—which (big mistake) left the powerful very powerful and the powerless very powerless—would continue through the birth and collapse of twenty-one mostly short-lived dynasties, until the weakened nation would be taken over by the Mongols (the Yüan Dynasty), taken back and stagnated by stodgy governing (the Ming Dynasty), and then taken over by the Manchus (the Ch'ing Dynasty). China would then be: conquered by the British, who forced the opium trade on the crippled nation; torn by riots and rebellions against the "Dragon Throne"; invaded by the Japanese; and then—after it had been reduced to debilitating poverty, mass starvation, and chaos by the Empress Dowager's self-centered mismanagement—taken over by the Communists.

But all that was yet to come. When the collection of verses later known as the *Tao Te Ching* was written, the Mongol takeover of China was *more than 1,600 years in the future*. At the time of the *Tao Te Ching*'s creation, Master K'ung had died, and his followers had not yet succeeded in spreading his teachings throughout every area and level of national and local government—and yet the author of the *Tao Te Ching* singled out *that one* of the era's Hundred Schools of philosophy to depict as a force that would cripple and stagnate the nation.

Reading the *Tao Te Ching* today, knowing what we now know about the history of China after its creation, it is easy to overlook the fact that the *Tao Te Ching* came first and the Confucianism we know about, the ruling religious/political system of China, came later. The author of the *Way Virtue Classic* was one of a small number of men in history gifted with, or cursed with, the ability to observe the beginnings of social phenomena and know where they will lead. Cursed, I say, because such people are destined to be ignored, disbelieved, and belittled by those around them who have no such ability. The majority of people in any society are carried along by social trends as leaves are carried along by the current of a stream. Later, with hindsight, they can look back and see that the prophets and their prophecies were correct. But by then, it is usually too late.

What I believe the author is saying here and there in his writing is that Master K'ung chose the wrong past to emulate. There was an *older* past, which, paradoxically, could have been built upon to help Chinese society move *forward*—a past in which people had lived in harmony with nature. In that time, people recognized that nature's wisdom and power were far greater than their own, so they aligned themselves with her and lived their lives accordingly, without the superimposed rules and regulations of a Confucian system. That was the time before The Great Way was abandoned.

In line one, "abandoned" is from *fei*, "to abandon," "ruined," "useless." The character depicts a house in ruins.

Regarding "clever Knowing" (*hui chih*) in line three: In the standard text, but not in some other texts, the *chih* used there and once in Chapter Nineteen is not the fitting-the-context Confucian principle *chih*, "knowing," "perception," or "wisdom," but is a structurally similar *chih* meaning "knowledge," "cleverness," or "wisdom," depending on context. The latter *chih*'s use in line three following *hui*, "intelligent," "clever," or "wise," produces—depending on how one interprets the combination—either a duplication of meanings or a denunciation of intelligence, cleverness, knowledge, or wisdom. Every translated standard-text *Tao Te Ching* interpretation that I checked went approximately like: "When intelligence and wisdom [or "knowledge"] arose [or "arise"], the great hypocrisy began [or "begins"]." Which has the author denouncing intelligence and wisdom (or knowledge).

It seemed clear to me that in the context of both this chapter and Chapter Nineteen the author is criticizing codified Confucian principles, rather than criticizing intelligence, wisdom, or knowledge. So I replaced the text's *chih* with the Confucian-principle *chih* and interpreted the resulting *hui chih* as "clever Knowing"—Knowing as practiced by the clever but not-so-wise Confucianists.

Accordingly, lines three and four are my interpretation of *hui* ("intelligent," "clever," or "wise") *chih* ("knowing," "perception," or "wisdom") *ch'u* ("arise," "come forth") *yu* ("have") *ta* ("great") *wei* ("false, counterfeit"): "Clever Knowing has arisen—we have a great falsehood."

My basic translation of the standard text of the chapter, with the Confucian-principle *chih*, "Knowing," substituted for *chih*, "knowledge," "cleverness," or "wisdom," was:

> Great Way abandon[ed]
> have Benevolence Righteousness
> clever Knowing arise[n]
> have great falsehood
> Six Relationships not harmonious
> have Filial Piety Maternal Affection
> nation['s] household dark disorder[ed]
> have Loyal Ministers

In contrast, the translations I've seen of the chapter are past or present-tense variations of:

> When the Great Way was abandoned,
> Then came forth benevolence and righteousness.
> When intelligence and wisdom [or knowledge] arose,
> Then great hypocrisy began.
> When the six relationships lost their harmony,
> Then were born filial piety and compassion.
> When the nation fell into darkness and disorder,
> Then loyal ministers appeared.

The long-accepted meaning of those interpretations is that when The Great Way was/is abandoned, benevolence and righteousness (not capitalized), which had gone unnoticed when the nation was healthy, became/become visible. And so on, down through the rest of the chapter's lines. But when applying that interpretation-meaning, lines three and four don't work—they don't fit the pattern of the rest. Also, it seems very odd that the author would be, in effect, endorsing or promoting Confucian codified principles (whether capitalized or not)—that he would imply that they were desirable and good. So I concluded that, as I believe my basic translation shows, the characters are saying something else—something *Taoist*, not *Confucianist*.

The characters, in their couldn't-be-simpler, grimly sarcastic way, tell what the author is seeing all around him: "The Great Way has been abandoned, family relations have lost their harmony, and a great falsehood has arisen. All that we have in place of what once existed are promoted codified principles known as 'Benevolence,' 'Righteousness,' 'Knowing,' 'Six Relationships,' 'Filial Piety,' 'Maternal Affection,' and 'Loyalty.'"

19.

SIMPLIFY

In the *Tao Te Ching*, the author writes in what could be called a loose style (lines of varying length) and in what could be called a tight style (lines of identical length). He often uses both in one chapter. For example, he may write a few lines of varying length followed by lines of identical length, the latter of which may or may not rhyme.

This chapter's text, as it exists today, consists of a section made up of five lines of eight characters each—if three necessary characters are inserted into obvious gaps in the five-character fifth line—followed by a section made up of two four-character lines. That much is easy enough to translate. But once one goes beyond a translate-the-characters acquaintance with the chapter—if one does go beyond it—one is bound to start seeing oddities in its first section.

The first one is that the rhyme scheme, which the author is clearly capable of managing, doesn't quite work. That scheme seems to consist of rhyming the fourth and eighth characters of each line with those of the other lines. But in the first line, neither the fourth nor the eighth character rhymes with those of the following lines. And in the fifth line, only one of the two ought-to-be-rhyming characters rhymes with those of the previous lines.

The second odd thing is the absence of the character *chiang* (indicates future action) from the first three lines. I added it to my interpretation as "will": "The people will benefit" (my line two), "The people will return" (my line four), and "Robbers and thieves will cease" (my line seven). All other interpretations I've seen also include "will," which is necessary for understandability. The addition of *chiang* makes the first three lines of the text nine, not eight, characters in length.

I wondered if someone had squeezed those lines down to their present length in order to match that of the others. I'd seen some signs of that sort of thing having been done in some other chapters. And that thought brought my attention to a third oddity:

The first two characters of the first line are *chüeh shêng*, "sever/destroy wise," at first glance meaning either "Get rid of the wise" or "Get rid of wisdom." All interpretations I've seen say something of the sort. But why would a writer who throughout his writing advocates *emulating* the wise and *applying* wisdom here advocate *eliminating* the wise or wisdom? The answer is: He doesn't. *Shêng*, "wise," is an adjective. It is used as such everywhere else in the *Tao Te Ching*, and is used as such today. It does not mean "the wise" or "wise men" (nouns) or "wisdom" (noun). The character for "wise man" or "wise men" is *hsien*, "wise man" or "venerable," not *shêng*. Did a copyist, I wondered, mistake the sound of the former for that of the latter? (The characters *look* completely different.) Then I considered that:

In this chapter and the previous one—despite what other interpreters and commentators say—the author clearly seems to be strongly criticizing Confucianism, the founder of which was, as I would put it, obsessed with the *shêng wang*, the "sage-kings" (more literally "wise kings") of Confucian tradition. So I concluded that the chapter's *shêng* was the first part of what was originally, and appropriately, *shêng wang*. The result of that conclusion was: "Eliminate Sage-Kings." Which made the first line of the text *ten* characters in length.

As I did in Chapter Eighteen, I replaced the standard text's *chih* ("knowledge," "cleverness," or "wisdom") in this chapter's first line with the structurally similar Confucian-principle *chih* ("knowing," "perception," or "wisdom") used in some other texts, as the latter seemed far more likely to have been what the author wrote. The translations/interpretations I've seen that were based on the standard text's *chih* ("knowledge," "cleverness," or "wisdom") present the first stanza's opening characters variously as "Get rid of sageliness, discard wisdom," "Eliminate wisdom, abandon cleverness," "Throw away wisdom, discard knowledge" (again having the author criticizing *knowledge*), and so on.

My translation of the text's second sentence, with the seemingly eliminated *chiang* added to it, was: "Sever/destroy Benevolence, discard Righteousness [—] the people will return [to] Filial Piety [and] Maternal Affection." Not satisfied with that recommendation to get rid of two Confucian codified principles in order to return to two other Confucian codified principles, which seemed ridiculous and out-of-character (were the suspicious-wording occurrences in the previous chapter and this one the work of a meddling Confucianist?), I turned the wording into: "Eliminate Filial Piety, discard Maternal Affection—the people will return to esteem-for-parents and motherly love." I hesitated to tamper with the text to that extent, but finally decided that the substitutions—which go along with the text of lines five and six of the previous chapter—worked much better than did the originals (if they *were* the originals, which I doubt).

In the second line of my second stanza, the character I (most likely uniquely) present as "strokes and lines" is *wên*, "strokes," "lines," "ornaments," "written characters," "written composition."

Most other interpreters of the four-character text of the last line of my third stanza place it according to tradition, at the beginning of Chapter Twenty. I placed it at the end of this chapter because, for one reason, it rhymes with the two four-character lines of the chapter's traditional ending. (The rhyming characters are the last in each line: *p'u*, line one; *yü*, line two; and *yu*, my line three.) For another reason, the text of my first stanza contains three recommendations, so those given in my third stanza ought to be three in number as well. For a third reason, when that line is used as the first line of Chapter Twenty, it doesn't fit.

20.
I ALONE

It's my opinion that the opening five statements of the Chinese text of Chapter Twenty don't belong there. The inclusion of the first one was seemingly done when the continuous text was divided into chapters (sections). It clearly belongs at the end of Chapter Nineteen, as I explained in the notes for that chapter, so I moved it there. The remaining four statements were, I believe, added by someone with a conspicuously different vocabulary. Their Philosophy 101 musings seem uncharacteristic of the author. So I left them out.

And now for the much-more-interesting material:

All of the English-language *Tao Te Ching* interpretations that I've seen have the author paint a grim portrait of himself in this chapter. He is, he tells us in those interpretations, stolid-faced, lazy, and just plain stupid. One might wonder: Is he incapable of accurate self-knowledge?

Previous English-language interpreters of Chapter Twenty have chosen to not include the second half of each of the repeated-character phrases—*lei lei* ("lazy-lazy"), *tun tun* ("chaos-chaos"), *hun hun* ("dim-dim") and so on. Possibly they considered those rather comical colloquialisms too undignified for the "Old Master" to use in a composition—even one as unusual as the *Tao Te Ching*—and dismissed them as being too "of the people." But their "of the people" nature seems to me to be the author's reason for using them. To explain what I'm getting at:

When those quirky phrases are included, a very different sort of self-portrait emerges: The author, far from seriously describing himself as a lazy simpleton, appears to be observing other people observing him, and is reporting, using their phrases, what sort of person they seem to be seeing—a lazy simpleton. And he appears to be having fun describing himself through their eyes, before stating something deeper about himself (third stanza, last three lines). To emphasize this initially through-others'-eyes approach to self-description, I put the descriptive phrases in quotation marks. And I put exclamation marks after "lazy-lazy" and "chaos-chaos," as the author uses an exclamation/emphasis character after each of those two pairs of characters.

To me, the most intriguing thing about the author's amused and amusing commentary is that it reveals how practiced he is at concealing his true self. He has a brilliant mind, but no ego. And that combination enables him to disguise his intelligence. He "hides in plain sight," like the ideal Taoist described by the Ch'in Dynasty Taoist alchemist Ko Hung:

> Many look at him, but nobody sees him. Calm and detached, he is free
> from all danger—a dragon hidden among men.

Regarding *i i* ("yee yee") in the text of my first stanza, first line, which I interpreted as "smiley-smiley": the standard text has *hsi hsi* instead. *Hsi*'s definitions, "glorious," "brilliant," "splendid," "ample," didn't seem to fit the context, so I consulted two other texts and in each case instead of *hsi* saw *i*, from which *hsi* differs by its inclusion of an abbreviated version of the character for "fire." The *i* in those other texts means "broad chin"—in this context, I believe, signifying *a chin broadened by a smile* (Warring States period slang, perhaps?). *Hsi* seems to have been a copying error.

"Anchored and fastened" in my first stanza's fourth line is my interpretation of *po*, "to moor," "to anchor," "to fasten" (more ancient slang?)—a character presented in other English-language editions that I've seen in a number of ways, but not as "moored," "anchored," or "fastened."

The character *t'ai*, which I present as "tower" in the third line of my first stanza, is typically presented in this chapter as "terrace," its later definition. Its ancient ancestor, which meant *tower* or *lookout*, depicted a lofty foundation supporting a high pavilion, on the roof of which birds are perching. Such structures, which were used for landscape viewing as well as for watchtowers, were common to the estates of wealthy nobles, as evidenced by tower models found during tomb excavations.

On the subject of *wealthy nobles*: Although the author indicates in this chapter that he hides his true self from those around him, he—unintentionally, I assume—gives the careful reader some clues about his social standing. I'll emphasize some words in the following quotations to show what I mean: "Many people are 'smiley-smiley' . . . *ascending the tower in spring*. . . . Many people *have all they need, and more*. . . . The *common people* 'look-look'; *I alone am 'hidden-hidden'* ["anchored and fastened" behind an impassive high-caste facade?]—*tranquil as the sea, constant as a high wind*."

"Hidden-hidden" in the above is from *pi*, "hidden," "secret." The brush-character used in the standard text of Chapter Twenty is *mên*, "depressed," "melancholy," or "stupid." But in the chapter's context, in which the author contrasts himself with the common people who "look-look" him over—literally "examine-examine" or "inspect-inspect"—*mên*'s "depressed" or "melancholy" doesn't work, and its "stupid" (which doesn't work, either) has been covered by the previous statement. According to analytical dictionaries, the similar character *pi* depicts an arrow dividing the number eight—signifying *certainty* or *the solution to a problem or doubt*—behind a gate. From which comes "hidden," "secret," "mysterious." A sloppy copyist, by leaving out one stroke, could duplicate the character *mên*, a heart/mind behind a gate—"depressed," "melancholy," or "stupid." When I considered the text of the next two lines, I concluded that *pi*, not *mên*, was likely the original brush-character.

If one takes an even closer look at the author's statements, one can notice what might be another, more subtle indication of his social status:

In contrast to the "smiley-smiley" people, the author says that he is (appears) emotionally "anchored and fastened." In contrast to the "bright-bright" people, he says that he is "dim-dim." In contrast to the curious "look-look" people, he says that he is "hidden-hidden." Therefore, in contrast to the people who "have all they need, and more," the expected statement would be that he has nothing. Instead, he states that he *appears abandoned* (*jo*, "resemble," "equal to," "to be as," "as if," followed by *i*, "left behind," "lost," "forgotten," later also meaning "to give, to bequeath"). Did someone miscopy some characters? Or—more likely, I think, considering the other clues—did the author catch himself about to write something inaccurate and untrue, something that no one observing him would have said, and as a result shift to another description of his appearance in order to contrast himself with the people mentioned? In this chapter, he is describing himself as *the opposite of* the various people he encounters. He's not a sloppy craftsman—so why would he break his pattern in that one instance, if not for the above reason?

The typical *Tao Te Ching* interpretation does not have the author say some equivalent of "I alone appear abandoned [left behind, lost, or forgotten]," but instead has him say "I alone have nothing," "I alone appear poor," or (in some cases) "I alone seem to have lost everything [or "lost out"]." Sometimes changing the wording of a passage to make the pattern of one statement match the pattern of the others can be an improvement. But sometimes doing so changes the substance of what the author apparently wrote. In this case, in my opinion, "improving" the wording leaves out something of possible significance revealed by the characters. Some English-language translations of the *Tao Te Ching* include the Chinese text. With these, in the text of this chapter—despite whatever their interpretations of the characters may say—the characters in question are clearly *wo tu jo i*, "I alone appear left behind/lost/forgotten."

"Tranquil" in my third stanza, line five, is from *tan*, "tranquil, calm," "dull." Many English-language versions have "drifting," "formless," "indifferent," "vague," and so on, thereby making the author define himself very differently than he does in the standard text and some others.

"Constant" in the following line is from the text's *liu hsi* (an emphasis/exclamation character) *jo wu chih*, "high-wind-like without stopping," or "like a *high wind*, without ceasing"—*liu*, a high wind, being one that keeps steadily, ceaselessly blowing because at a high altitude it meets no obstruction. In many interpretations, the phrase becomes "without direction, like the restless wind," "aimless, like a wandering wind," and the like—all of which, again, create a very different self-description.

Possibly some of the interpretations mentioned in the two previous paragraphs were based on the characters in the Ma-wang-tui texts. Those texts, which I quickly learned not to trust—see my notes for Chapter Thirty-One—have *hu*, "formless," and *huang*, "shapeless," instead of *tan*, "tranquil," and *liu*, "high wind," as in the standard text and others, thereby having the author say that he is "formless as the sea" and "shapeless, without resting." But is the sea *formless*? Is the author—or anyone else—*shapeless*?

In my fourth stanza, "And yet I appreciate being fed by our Mother" is my version of *erh kuei shih mu*:

then/and yet/and/but   value/appreciate   food/to feed/fed   mother

Despite the lack of an equivalent of capital letters in Chinese—and despite the statement's apparent shortage of characters—it's easy to deduce that the "mother" mentioned is The Mother of the Ten Thousand Things.

I eliminated a part of the text that would have followed the third stanza of my interpretation. It was redundant, and suspect, in two ways: It repeated the text of the first two lines of my second stanza, except for a different final character; and it went back to the "I seem stupid" theme after the author had dropped it and had gone on to something more revealing. It had him say that he is "stupid/doltish/ignorant [*wan*], like [a] rustic [*ssu pi*]." Elsewhere in the chapter for "like," "as," "as if," or "as when," the author uses *ju* (three times) and *jo* (four times), but not *ssu*. *Wan* and *pi*, I determined by scanning, are not used anywhere else in the *Tao Te Ching*. And, tellingly, the segment lacked the doubled-character ironic humor of the author's self-deprecating remarks. It appeared to me to be the work of someone who didn't grasp what the author had been saying in his subtle way—that he hid behind a "mask"—and who felt compelled to heavy-handedly restate the "I seem stupid" theme. But he restated it in an inappropriate place, interrupting the progression from "I alone [am] 'hidden-hidden'"—or (redundantly) "stupid-stupid," using the dubious *mên*—to "And yet [I] appreciate [being] fed [by our] Mother." So, as I see it, *the interrupter* was "stupid/doltish/ignorant," not the author.

Finally, "go" in my first stanza's last line is my in-context interpretation of *kuei*, which can mean "return home," "go back" *or* "go to," "go toward a goal." "Go to" seemed the obvious meaning.

"*'Lazy-lazy!' as if I have nowhere to go.*" Do the author's slangy self-descriptions in this chapter create a picture of an Old Master? Or do they perhaps create a picture of a secretive, daydreaming young nobleman with plenty of time on his hands? I'll have more on the latter further on.

21.
SOMETHING ELUSIVE

Chapter Twenty-One includes a character very important in Taoism: *te*, traditionally translated somewhat inadequately as "virtue." It's commonly capitalized in English-language translations because of its next-to-*tao* prominence in the *Tao Te Ching*. *Te* consists of the character for "upright" joined to that for "heart," the combination meaning "virtue," "nobility of character," or, in jazz slang, "soul"—an "upright heart." After the time of the writing of the *Way Virtue Classic*, the character for "left foot," signifying *stepping out*, was added, forming the compound character *te*, "upright heart in action." In this presentation, only the original definition applies—although, to my way of thinking, the later character's meaning already existed as part of its ancestor's. After all, what would virtue or any other attribute be without action to put it into effect?

Every interpretation of this chapter seems to present a different version of its opening statement. The following are my translations of the characters, the first of which gives the ancient meaning of *k'ung*. In English word-order, "only" would be the first word and "Way" would be the last.

> the hidden recess of swallow-nestlings Virtue 's countenance only
>   Way exactly follows

Other interpretations of the text of my second stanza leave out *chih* (possessive sign) and *wei* ("action[s]") from the phrase *tao chih wei* ("[The] Way's actions") in the text of my first line, or interpret *wei* as "character," producing a first sentence like "The Way's nature is uncertain and intangible" or "The Way is something elusive and obscure." But with The Way as the subject, the sentences after that one don't make sense.

In various lines of the second stanza, I interpreted *huang*, "uncertain," as "elusive." The latter seemed more appropriate in context.

The text of the third through eighth lines of the stanza has emphasis/exclamation characters after certain characters. In each case, I moved the emphasis to the next line down, where I thought it worked better in English. For example: In the text of my third line, *hu* ("obscure") and *huang* ("uncertain" or "elusive") are emphasized. I shifted the emphasis to *hsian* ("image") in the following line. In the text of my tenth line, I added emphasis to *hsin* ("sincerity").

In the stanza's fourth-from-last line, I interpreted *ming* as "renown," a synonym of the definition "fame," rather than as the definition "name" found in other interpretations.

22.
ADHERING TO THE ONE

After I'd figured out from the text of my final stanza's first two lines that the text of what is now my second stanza was (allegedly) an ancient saying, I preceded that ancient-saying stanza with one of my devising, for clarity.

The difference between most interpretations I've read of the characters of my second stanza and my own interpretation comes down to: Does (in line two, for example) *wang tsai ch'üan*, "crooked then straight," mean "The crooked shall then be straight"? Does it mean "Make yourself crooked and you shall then be straight"? Or (the most popular choice) does it mean "Bend and be straightened" or an equivalent?

I believe the answer is in the text of the first three lines of the stanza that follows the saying. Its characters are: *shih i* ("so," "therefore," or "rightly and accordingly") *shêng jên* ("wise man") *pao* ("embraces," "holds tightly") *i* ("one" or, in this context, "The One") *wei* ("becoming," "being") *t'ien hsia* ("heaven under") *shih* ("pattern"). By making oneself crooked, is one holding tightly to The One and becoming under-heaven's pattern? It seems to me that the saying simply means that the crooked shall then become straight—or the carpenters' equivalent that I used, "true."

Following the characters of my ancient-saying stanza were some that I translated as: "[The] few [shall] then obtain; [the] many [shall] then [be] misled." (The typical interpretation presents these as: "Have little and gain; have much and be confused," or the like—which neither follows the characters nor fits the context.) Those characters, which didn't fit the defective-set-right pattern established by the ones before them, seemed to have been added by another writer with another agenda. I thought they distracted from, rather than added to, the saying; so I eliminated them.

For an explanation of why the wording of my third stanza's lines eight through eleven differs significantly from that of other versions, see my notes on Chapter Twenty-Four, in which similar statements appear.

The incomplete-seeming five-character text of my final stanza's last line has been interpreted in many ways, often by leaving out or redefining a character or two. I chose what seemed the simplest interpretation:

[Be] truly (*ch'êng*) whole (*ch'üan*) and (*erh*) return (*kuei*) [to] them (*chih*).

23.
SWIRLING WINDS, SWIFT RAIN

Regarding "how much truer that is" in the eighth line of my first stanza: I looked up that line's second character, *k'uang*, in classical Chinese dictionaries and read "ice water." In another edition of the standard *Tao Te Ching*, I found the same character and the same definition. I checked the text of a third standard edition and saw a slightly different *k'uang*, the dictionary definitions of which were "moreover," "furthermore," and "how much the more then"—obviously the appropriate meanings. Which shows that a slight mistake in selecting a character to print can turn *moreover*, *furthermore*, and *how much the more then* into *ice water*. It also shows that a mistake in one publication can be duplicated in another, demonstrating the danger of playing follow-the-leader.

In the ninth line of the first stanza, I added "the windy jabbering of" to clarify what I believe the author is saying. Some interpretations of the stanza's characters seem to be based on the belief that the "swirling winds" (*p'iao fêng*) and "swift rain" (*chou yü*) of lines two and four represent violent activity that could be compared to man's, rather than nature's rare equivalent of strenuous verbosity. So instead of something like "windy jabbering" those interpretations say something like "violent actions." But the opening characters—*hsi yen tzǔ jan*, "rare/seldom words [are] in accordance with nature"—point in another direction.

Throughout the *Tao Te Ching*, the author advocates quiet, subtle, egoless action in harmony with The Way in order to change things for the better. In this first stanza, he seems to be criticizing the noisy Confucianists and other spokesmen for the era's Hundred Schools of philosophy, all of whom are working hard to persuade rulers to adopt their systems of government—and are likely wearing themselves down in the process. "So," concludes the author, "be one who follows and works with The Way."

Regarding the word *error* in my second and third stanzas: *Shih* is defined as "to lose," "to slip," "to err." Other interpretations of the chapter tend to render *shih* as "loss." But to me "error" seemed a more appropriate choice.

The text of my second stanza, in my interpretation, reads:

way one who join[ed] with way
virtue one who join[ed] with virtue
error one who join[ed] with error

In English-language word order, "Way one who" would be "One who [is of The] Way," and so on.

The text of my third stanza has been interpreted in many ways. Its first sentence can serve to show the structure of all three in the stanza:

joins with Way one who Way in fact glad to receive him

Following the text of my three stanzas was a sentence identical to one in Chapter Seventeen. It fit better there than it did here, so I eliminated it.

In this chapter, the author personifies error as welcoming the erring individual: "Error is truly [literally "in fact"] glad to receive him." In Chapter Thirty-Eight, he personifies Confucian High Propriety: "High Propriety strives for [Virtue], and negatively it responds—so High Propriety grabs it by the arm, and throws it away." There's something of Lewis Carroll's humor in that.

An element that from the beginning has distinguished Taoism from other spiritual teachings is: a sense of humor. And although that element has been overlooked by the scholars who have interpreted and commented on the *Way Virtue Classic*, it is present in the text just the same—as can be seen by revisiting Chapter Twenty:

My mind is that of a simpleton: "chaos-chaos!"

The common people are "bright-bright"; I alone am "dim-dim."

I alone differ from the rest—and yet I appreciate being fed by our Mother.

24.
USELESS ACTION

In the last two statements of the first stanza, "punishes himself" and "pities himself" are my versions of *tzŭ fa*, "self chastise," and *tzŭ ching*, "self pity." All English-language versions I've seen of this chapter and of Chapter Twenty-Two, in which the same character-combinations occur, take the opposite approach: Instead of "punishes himself" and "pities himself," they say "promotes himself" and "praises himself," or their equivalents.

At least at first glance, those push-and-boast interpretations make more sense than do more literal ones, even though the characters do say what they say. In a situation like this, one can either change the meanings of the characters in order to make them make sense (the all-too-typical approach) or (my first step) try to see if there might be sense in what they are saying. After reflecting on the text's statements for a while, I concluded that in the case of "He who punishes himself will not have merit" and "He who pities himself will not grow," the author is dealing with some surprisingly modern psychology principles—too modern, I think, for the early, trend-setting interpreters of the *Tao Te Ching*. And I realized that in either promoting or punishing oneself, and in either praising or pitying oneself, the focus is on oneself. If one can "submerge" the self (see Chapter Thirteen and my notes on Chapter Sixteen) or at least be neutral about it, the self fades into the background and one can focus attention on other matters.

Happy children do this; unhappy children do not. I believe that is what the characters are saying.

25.
IN THE SILENCE

My first stanza's interpretation started out as printed in part at the beginning of this book—as faithful as possible to the Chinese text. But I soon found myself rhyming the words in the spirit of the various rhythms and rhymes that pop up here and there throughout the work. When I had finished the final draft, I looked at what I'd written and thought: What have I done? I've turned one of the most profound sections of the *Tao Te Ching* into the equivalent of a Madison Avenue soap advertisement! And then I could have sworn that I heard a young male voice laughing and saying, "Now you've got it! *That's* the idea!" So I kept the stanza as I'd modified it.

In the rhyming process, I added "was born," "spinning round," "did it bring," "of Everything," "If I were," and "I would." Also, I reversed the halves of each of the text's first two statements, which translate as:

existed thing turbid completed before heaven earth birth
silence ! emptiness ! alone stood not changing

"Word" in the first stanza's next-to-last line is my in-that-context interpretation of *ming*, "name," "title." In ancient China, according to my research, *ming*, "name," and characters meaning "word," such as *yen*, were often interchangeable in meaning. "Give a word for it" seemed more appropriate in that line than "give a name for it," considering that the author has already told us in this chapter—as he does elsewhere—that he does not know the name of what he calls The Way.

My second stanza touches on the subject of *returning*, which both the author and I address more fully elsewhere.

Following the text of my second stanza were characters for another one:

Therefore:
The Way is great,
Heaven is great,
Earth is great,
And the king is great.
Within this territory
We have four greats,
And the king resides
As its *number-one.*

I removed that traditionally included stanza because it read like something irrelevant to the subject at hand that someone patriotically—or, I suspect, *anti*-patriotically as a criticism of a conceited king—inserted into the text in response to *ta*, "great," in the material before it.

Regarding that stanza's last two lines: Other interpretations I've seen say "and the king is one of them," or the like. But that's not what I believe is being said. The characters in question are *erh wang chü ch'i i yen*, which I translated as:

> and   king/ruler   occupies the position [of]   its [the territory's]
>   number-one   why?/final affirmative/emphasis

26.
THE WISE PRINCE

The standard text of this chapter is supposedly concerned with the journey of a *shêng jên*, a "wise man," designated as such in the text of my first stanza's fifth line. That designation makes for a very strange narrative, referring as the chapter does to this individual as the "lord of ten thousand warrior-wagons"—"warrior-wagon" being my translation of *chêng*, a roofed vehicle for transporting warriors standing back-to-back in two ranks. By description, the journey is hardly one made by a *shêng jên*, a "wise man." Did someone copying the text make a substantial mistake? Some texts have *chün tzŭ*, "princely master" or "sovereign master," rather than *shêng jên*.

In his 1891 work, *The Texts of Taoism* (republished in 1962 by Dover Publications, New York), James Legge, who for twenty years held the chair in Chinese Language and Culture at Oxford University, substituted "wise prince" for "wise man" in his interpretation of and comments on this chapter. He based the substitution on a commentary on the chapter traditionally attributed to the Warring States period philosopher/ prince Han Fei-tzŭ (280? BCE–233 BCE). I adopted that substitution—despite the fact that scholars now consider the commentary to have probably been written later, by scholars of the Ch'in Dynasty or early Han Dynasty—because the individual in question is by description a prince.

The text of the chapter's first sentence is *chung wei ch'ing kên*, "Heaviness acts [as] lightness['s] root." That phrasing seemed ambiguous to me—it could be read as meaning that lightness grows from heaviness. So I changed "root" to "anchor" in both the first and second stanzas.

The text of the second sentence is *ching wei tsai chün*, "Stillness acts [as] hastiness['s] sovereign." The author's use there of *chün*, "sovereign," lays the foundation for a play on words in the chapter's final sentence, *tsao tsê shih chün*: "[If he were to be] hasty [,] then [he would] lose [his] sovereign"—the prince's rash behavior would not only sever his connection to hastiness's *sovereign*, stillness, it would also cost him the support of his *sovereign*, the king.

In my first stanza, I added "as he goes on his way" (second-to-last line). Aside from that addition and my two previously mentioned substitutions—"anchor "for "root" and "wise prince" for "wise man"—my wording choices, different though some of them are from other versions, follow the characters closely.

27.
SUBTLETY

Until I examined the Chinese text, I believed that two of its claims were nonsense. The interpretations I'd read told me that a well-closed door or a good closer of doors needs no lock, yet the door closed cannot be opened; and that a good binding or binder needs no knots, yet the binding cannot be loosened.

Then I looked at the characters and checked their definitions. I saw that instead of "lock," the character *kuan* is defined as "crossbar of a gate"—and therefore the object being closed is a *gate*. Instead of "knots," I saw, the character *shêng* means "cord" or "string." The sentences (lines four through nine of my first stanza) became more believable.

Regarding "skilled," my interpretation of *shan*: In this chapter's context, *shan* would mean either morally good ("good," "kind," "honest," "virtuous") or well-skilled ("skillful, dexterous"). The latter is what the chapter seemed to be about. Most of the interpreters whose versions I checked used "good": "A good man is the teacher [*shih*, "master"] of a bad man," etc.

My first stanza's last line is my substitute for the text's *ku*, "so" or "therefore." I wanted to better communicate the point that the author seems to be making, that the greatest skills make use of subtlety. In line six of my second stanza, I added "subtlety of the wise" for the same reason.

The characters for the last two lines of my second stanza are shih ("this") *wei* ("called") *hsi* ("cloak," "overcoat") *ming* ("light, brightness"). Every interpretation that I checked seemed different. The only one like what I came up with was that by James Legge: "This is called 'Hiding the light of his procedure.'" Relative to that interpretation, he writes in his notes for the chapter that "The action of the Tao (non-acting and yet all-efficient) and that of the sage in accordance with it are veiled by their nature from the sight of ordinary men." Because of their *subtlety*.

In my third stanza, line seven, "clever" is my interpretation of *chih*, "knowledge-able," "clever," or "wise," depending on context.

The last four words of my final stanza are my interpretation of *yao miao*. *Yao* is defined as "to "want, to wish" "to seek," "to strive for," "to exact," "to coerce." After a good deal of trying this or that, I settled on "to strive for," "to coerce [force]." *Miao* as used in the *Tao Te Ching* means either "mystery" or "subtlety," depending on context. I chose "subtlety" here; other interpretations I've seen use "mystery" or an equivalent. So my interpretation of *yao miao* was "struggling for the subtlety." If master/apprentice relations are strained (my third stanza's lines five through eight), teaching and learning a skill become a matter of striving, struggling, or forcing—not *wu wei*, and not the way to reach the highest skill level, that which makes use of subtlety.

Another way of expressing the above principle is the following, from the book *The Genius of Japanese Carpentry: Secrets of an Ancient Craft*, by Azby Brown (Tuttle Publishing, Rutland, Vermont, 2013):

> A master lacking compassion will be unable to shape his workers' thinking in a way that will enable them to successfully execute the highest quality work.

28.

CONSTANT VIRTUE
NATURAL SIMPLICITY

This chapter covers a lot of territory in a small space. It urges readers to: favor *yin* nurturing, gentleness, and modesty; live in a state of Constant Virtue; set a positive example; govern with simplicity; and always *return*—to a childlike state, to Natural Simplicity, to The Origin of Everything.

I made a separate section of what was going to be the chapter's fourth stanza because, even though it appeared to me to have been inspired in the author's mind by his previous sentence, it has a different focus: *p'u*, Natural Simplicity, rather than the *ch'ang te*, Constant Virtue, of the preceding stanzas. I'll describe *p'u* a bit further on.

In my first section, I emphasized the sentence-repetitions because the sentences seemed to have been repeated to emphasize their images.

Although I translated/interpreted the first section's text as literally as I could, I transformed its *pai*, "white" or "bright," and *hei*, "black" or "dark," in the second stanza's first statement into "brilliance" and "shadow," the latter of those two words in keeping with the chapter's *yin* theme (the character *yin* depicts the shaded side of a hill).

"The Origin of Everything," the last words of my first section's second stanza, is my interpretation of *wu chi*. *Wu* in this case means "Non-Being" or "Nothingness;" *chi*, as in *t'ai chi*, means "Ultimate" or "Highest." So *wu chi* could be translated as "Non-Being Ultimate," "Ultimate Emptiness," or "Highest Nothingness." *Wu chi* is the author's apparently original name for the spiritual origin of everything. One could describe *wu chi* as the pre-heaven Way of Heaven.

P'u, the last character in the text of my first section's third stanza, is an important term in Taoist philosophy. The classical dictionary definitions are: "Wood in its natural state, not worked," "rough," "plain," "natural," "normal," "simple." The character depicts a tree in a thicket. It's used to mean *natural simplicity*, of people or of things. *P'u* is often presented in Taoist writings—but not in the *Tao Te Ching*—as the "uncarved block."

The following is my character-by-character translation of the text of the second section:

> natural simplicity   breaks up   then   becomes   utensils
> wise   man   uses   it   then   becomes   official   excellent
> therefore   great   system   not   cut/reduced

In ancient China, the character *ch'i*—"utensils" in the first line of the above—had a double meaning. Then, as now, it meant "utensils," "instruments," or "vessels." But it was also a slang term for governmental lackeys, political or other operators, technical specialists, soldiers, and low-ranking employees. The author seems to be saying that the governing system advocated by the Confucianists would excessively cubbyhole its personnel into isolated, limiting, specialist-focus positions in the rigid Confucian political hierarchy, producing a "cut-up" (fragmented) government, while the more holistic, interdisciplinary thinking of the wise—which operates with the efficiency of nature's interactions—would produce a better system, one of organic wholeness.

For a relatively recent example of the latter-mentioned whole-government principle, consider the interdisciplinary thinking of President John F. Kennedy and the diversified, bipartisan council he assembled to arrive at a solution to the Cuban Missile Crisis.

In the text of the second section's final sentence, *chih* not only means "system," it also means "to cut and pare." So the author is not only saying, "A great system is one that has not been cut up or reduced to 'utensils,'" he's also slyly saying, "A great cut-and-parer does not cut." In other words, a great simplifier (which is what Master K'ung in his rigid way had been trying to be) does not fragment what he's simplifying.

29.
SACRED VESSEL

Look deep into nature, and then you will understand everything better.
ALBERT EINSTEIN

I believe in God, only I spell it Nature.
FRANK LLOYD WRIGHT

To a reasoning being, an act that accords with Nature is an act that accords
with reason.
MARCUS AURELIUS

Depending on context, the phrase "under heaven" in the *Tao Te Ching* can be inter-
preted as meaning either the physical world—the world of the ten thousand things—or,
on occasion, the sociopolitical realm. I chose what seemed here the obvious meaning.
The alternative simply didn't work.

Nowhere in Taoism is there a stronger belief in and emphasis on the principle
of *wu wei*, "without forcing" or "without fussing with," than in the matter of respecting
nature, the realm of The Valley Spirit.

In my first stanza's first sentence, "take hold of" is from *ch'ü*, "seize, take hold of."
The character depicts a hand grasping an ear. "Manage" is one of the basic definitions
of *wei*, "do," "act," "practice," "manage," "cause." I added the emphasis.

The text of my second sentence compares the world to a *shên ch'i*, a "sacred
vessel"—a temple vessel, which is to be handled with the greatest reverence and care.
"Tamper with" in that sentence and the next is my in-context interpretation of *wei*. "Not
get away with" is from *pu k'o*, "not [be] able to," "not [be] permitted to."

Between the sections of text that I made into my first and second stanzas was
what I would call an interruption, seventeen characters obviously (to me, at least) added
by a smaller-caliber writer with a uselessly speculating mind—possibly the author of the
Philosophy 101 musings that I eliminated from the traditional beginning of Chapter
Twenty. The statements they formed were awkward and weak, and their relevance to
the rest of the chapter was beyond my ability to perceive. Other interpreters have done
what they could to make them work, producing a variety of interesting statements by
way of a good deal of creative rewriting. But to me they were inferior and an interrup-
tion, so I left them out.

Whoever tampers with it will ruin it.

A fool sees not the same tree that a wise man sees.
WILLIAM BLAKE

The best friend on earth of man is the tree.
FRANK LLOYD WRIGHT

Protecting the world's forests represents perhaps the greatest and most cost-effective opportunity to turn the corner on climate change over the next two decades.

DR. STEVE SCHWARTZMAN Senior Director for Tropical Forest Policy, Environmental, Defense Fund

The best time to plant a tree is twenty years ago. The second-best time is *now*.

ANCIENT CHINESE SAYING

Trees absorb carbon dioxide and release oxygen—therefore, the fewer trees, the more carbon dioxide and the less oxygen. Learn from nature; work with nature—then the best solutions to problems will present themselves, because they'll come from the greatest problem-solver in existence. No one beats nature at her own game. Those are simple principles, easy to learn. Maybe it's time we started learning them.

And maybe it's time to recognize and appreciate what nature, through trees, can do:

Trees improve water quality by removing harmful chemicals from the soil, by filtering out toxins from rain and snow melt, and by reducing runoff, erosion, and flooding. Over one half of the nation's drinking water originates in forests, nature's water-purifying stations. According to the U.S. Environmental Protection Agency, it's far more economical to invest in healthy watersheds than to invest in human-engineered water-problem solutions. For every 10 percent increase in a watershed's forest cover, there is a 20 percent decrease in water-treatment costs.

Trees appropriately placed around buildings can reduce air-conditioning needs by 30 percent and save 20 to 50 percent in heating-energy costs. The cooling effect of one tree planted in the right place near a house is the equivalent of ten single-room air conditioners running twenty hours per day. Planting an average of four trees per house would produce an annual reduction of power-plant carbon emissions from 16,000 tons to 9,000 tons.

According to the National Wildlife Federation in 2018, there are two hundred million spaces along America's city streets in which trees could be planted. Making use of them would absorb thirty-three million more tons of carbon dioxide every year and save $4 billion in energy costs.

The planting of trees in cities has been shown to turn "bad" (high crime, low employment) neighborhoods into good neighborhoods. Trees clearly have a positive, calming influence on people. Baltimore, for example, experienced a 12 percent drop in outdoor crime for every 10 percent of tree-canopy increase. Communities with denser tree canopies tend to have higher all-around employment rates.

As for city tree-related employment: Urban tree planting produces employment opportunities that cannot be shipped overseas, such as for arborists, urban foresters, landscapers, tree pruners, and miscellaneous personnel. In one year, urban forestry in California supported 60,067 jobs, resulting in approximately $3.3 million in individual income.

Most urgently and importantly, trees are all that's keeping our extremely over-populated species and our dangerously overheated planet alive.

It will seem as though Nature should extinguish the human race, for it will be useless to the world and will bring destruction to all beings.
LEONARDO DA VINCI

Some related facts:

Carbon dioxide levels worldwide have reached 415 parts-per-million for the first time in millions of years.

A recent report from the World Health Organization estimates that around nine out of ten people live in areas with excessive air pollution.

Several thousand trees are becoming extinct.

U.S. Forest Service researchers have found that American cities and towns are losing around thirty-six million trees annually. Every mega-storm that hits an American city or town raises the number.

The economic loss from the decline in urban tree cover has been estimated at around $100 million annually.

The Forest Service has stated that "Urban deforestation compares with what's going on in the world's rain forests."

Redwood forests absorb more carbon dioxide than any other trees on Earth—up to ten times more than has been documented with tropical rain forests. But 95 percent of the redwoods have been cut down. Survivors that didn't burn in the recent firestorms are dying because of the rising heat.

Old-growth forests are much more efficient than younger ones at capturing carbon and generating oxygen. But few old-growth forests remain. In Canada, the world's largest intact old-growth forest is being clear-cut—at the rate of one million acres each year—and turned into toilet paper and other throwaway paper products. That boreal forest stores nearly twice as much carbon as exists in all of Earth's oil reserves. Northern forests replanted after clear-cutting often don't regrow, often fail to provide suitable habitat for threatened species, and retain less carbon. Canada's boreal forest provides homes for endangered species and sanctuaries for an estimated three-to-five billion birds, some of which migrate from as far away as Argentina. Its rich peat soils and intricate web of root-systems keep more than two hundred billion tons of carbon out of our planet's atmosphere. In addition, that forest contains some of the world's largest supplies of fresh water.

Climate scientists have stated that deforestation contributes more to pollution and global "warming" (overheating) than do emissions from the world's cars, trucks, trains, airplanes, and ships combined.

Yet the news media (favoring the timber industry?) consistently ignore such statements and instead state and imply that auto and truck emissions are the number-one culprit. The media also (favoring electric-power companies and manufacturers?) overlook the fact that electric cars, called "zero-emissions" vehicles, are in effect mostly coal-burners, as the major source of electrical energy in the industrialized world is still coal-fired plants—and coal-burning is a far worse source of planetary overheating than are auto and truck emissions. And the media (favoring the shipping industry?) totally ignore ships. "Poor regulation at Chinese ports is allowing one container ship to pollute as much as five hundred thousand trucks in a single day," according to David Pettit, Director of Southern California Air Program at Natural Resources Defense Council. The five hundred thousand figure is not a misprint.

The tropical and temperate forests of Australia are some of the world's most biologically diverse regions, home to more than 150 species of mammals, amphibians, reptiles, and birds, and to thousands of plant species found nowhere else on Earth. Today the continent's forests—those that didn't burn in the recent terrible fires—are being clear-cut for livestock and agriculture. As a result, sediment, fertilizer, and pesticides are running into the Great Barrier Reef, smothering coral reefs and polluting fragile marine ecosystems.

Indonesia's rain forests, the third largest rain-forest region on Earth, are being burned and clear-cut to make room for corporate palm oil plantations. The forests include carbon-rich peatland, which stores carbon equivalent to six times that released every year by fossil fuels. Indonesian rain forests house some of the world's most critically endangered species, including all three kinds of orangutans (80 percent of their habitat has been altered or lost) and the Sumatran tiger, now close to extinction. Indonesia now has more threatened and endangered species than are found in any other country on our planet, due to habitat destruction. Since 2012, 146 football-field areas of its rain forest have been burned or cut every hour. Similar devastation is taking place in Malaysia.

In the Brazilian Amazon, deforestation increased by over 70 percent between 2012 and 2018, as wealthy landowners and multinational corporations clear-cut and burned the irreplaceable rain forests—once they're destroyed they do not regenerate—to make way for corporate coffee and palm oil plantations, farms to grow soy destined for

China, and huge cattle ranches. (Cattle belch enormous quantities of methane, which scientists say is more harmful to Earth than the carbon dioxide emitted by automobiles.) Nearly two million acres of Brazilian rain forest were cleared in 2018. Every week now (2020), another forty square miles are burned. Brazil's president has strongly stated his approval.

Forty percent of the world's oxygen is supplied by rain forests. Rain forests are home to 50 percent of all the plant and animal species on Earth. Seventy percent of plants identified by the National Cancer Institute as useful in the treatment of cancer are found in rain forests.

Back in the United States of America:

Investigations have determined that four out of five forest fires are being caused by humans, through carelessness–cigarettes, fireworks, driving over dry grass (no more ecologically irresponsible truck and SUV commercials, please), abandoned campfires, poor power-line maintenance, and so on–as well as by deliberate fire-starting. In a recent television interview, a park ranger stated that a sizeable part of each of his fire-season workdays consists of extinguishing poorly doused or abandoned-while-burning campfires.

Many forests have burned so badly that they cannot regenerate themselves, and so must be replanted. But the United States is millions of acres behind in reforestation. The Forest Service budget, which includes money for some of that, is now dominated by the great expense of fighting forest fires. In 1991, 13 percent of its budget was spent on "wildfire suppression." Estimates indicate that by 2025, two-thirds of its budget will be spent on fighting fires, at an estimated cost of $1.8 billion.

The traditional replanting of burned or clear-cut forests with only marketable-timber trees of only one species ("monoculture") weakens forests by encouraging disease and insect infestations–now more than ever as the planet overheats.

A forest is far more than trees, as a city is far more than buildings. Clear-cutting a forest destroys all the life within it, from microorganisms and nutrients that keep the soil forest-friendly to the countless forms of life that live among and depend on trees. Clear-cutting a forest is the ecological equivalent of bombing a city into rubble.

Alone, out of all the animal species on Earth, our species–*Homo sapiens*, the self-proclaimed "wise man"–has squandered the natural resources that Earth has provided in abundance. Now our species is finally paying the price. But, unfairly, so are all the other species–what remains of them–who have worked *with* nature and by so doing have helped to keep the world alive. Will we not-so-wise beings learn from what *Homo sapiens* has done–or is it all for nothing?

If you possess a desire
To take hold of the world
And *manage* it,
I see that you will not get
What you wanted.
The world is a sacred vessel—
You will not get away with
Tampering with it.
Whoever tampers with it
Will ruin it.
Whoever grasps it
Will lose it.

Therefore, the wise
Discard the excessive,
Discard the extravagant,
Discard the extreme.

30.
THORNS AND BRAMBLES

In the Chinese text, the phrase *t'ien hsia*, "under heaven," appears after the characters of my first stanza's third line. I eliminated it as being awkward and unnecessary in English.

In my first stanza, the second sentence, "Military affairs are fond of rebounding and retaliation," is my interpretation of *ch'i* ("its") *shih* ("affairs") *hao* ("fond of," "love"–the character depicts a woman and her child) *huan* ("return," "repay," "recoil, rebound, retaliate"). Here and there in the chapters, the author personifies principles, ideas, and actions, giving them lives and wills of their own. This appeared to be one of those instances. The sentence seems to have about as many interpretations as there are versions of the *Tao Te Ching*.

In my second stanza, third line, "violence" is my interpretation of *kan*, dictionary-defined as "daring, boldness." The ancient ancestor of *kan* depicts a whip-holding hand striking a bear. I used the same pictographic reading of the character in Chapter Sixty-Four and Chapter Seventy-Three, as I explain in my notes on the latter. In each case, "violence" made a good deal more sense than did "daring" or "boldness."

In my second stanza, I rearranged the order of the five statements in lines five through fourteen for what I thought was better continuity. Their original order was 2, 5, 4, 3, 1.

In the sixth line of my second stanza, "destroy" is my interpretation of *fa*, "cut down," "chastise," "destroy." Other interpretations tend to present *fa* in this case as "brag" or "boast," even though "brag" or "boast" was covered by what then was the previous sentence, which is now the final one.

Following the text of my second stanza was a twelve-character section almost identical in characters, and identical in meaning, to one at the end of Chapter Fifty-Five (my third stanza of that chapter). The section's statements fit perfectly in the latter's context; but in my opinion they didn't fit in this chapter, so I eliminated them.

When a great army passes, a lean year surely follows.

In around 500 BCE, not long before the start of the Warring States period, a brief treatise on military strategy was allegedly written by a military tactition named Sun Wu. Circulated since its appearance under the title *Sun-tzŭ*, the work has come to be known in English as *The Art of War*.

Master Sun seems to have been a rather shadowy figure—though not as shadowy as "Master Lao," whose very shadow seems to have been manufactured. As is the case with the latter, the historian Ssu-ma Ch'ien recorded as authentic a dubious, fiction-like account of Master Sun, which scholars over the years have come to discount. (Strike two for Ssu-ma Ch'ien.) In historical reality, there did exist a general named Sun Wu, but very little is known about him. Whether he was the author of the *Sun-tzŭ* is open to question.

Many of the principles and tactics described in *The Art of War* can be applied today, and may therefore be considered timeless. But the cautionary statements made in the work, overlooked though they often are, may also be considered timeless. The following such statements are from the second chapter, known in English as "Waging War" (Lionel Giles, translator):

> [I]f the campaign is protracted, the resources of the state will not be equal to the strain.

> Contributing to maintain an army at a distance causes the people to be impoverished.

> With this loss of substance and exhaustion of strength, the homes of the people will be stripped bare, and three-tenths of their income will be dissipated; while government expenses . . . will amount to four-tenths of its total revenue.

> There is no instance of a country having benefitted from prolonged warfare.

According to *Mother Jones* magazine (2017):

[S]pending on war . . . takes up more than half of all federal discretionary funds and a fifth of total federal spending.

The Pentagon controls 70 percent of the federal government's $1.8 trillion in property, land, and equipment.

The Pentagon holds more than 80 percent of the federal government's inventories, including $6.8 billion of excess, obsolete, or unserviceable stuff.

According to the American Friends Service Committee (2019):

The United States is budgeting to spend $717 billion of your tax dollars on the military this year. That's about $1.4 million spent *every single minute* for war and so-called defense. It's about as much as is spent on the world's next fifteen largest militaries *combined*.

31.
WEAPONS AND WAR

A number of scholars have expressed doubts about the authenticity of this chapter. They point out that the Wang Pi edition of the *Tao Te Ching* lacks a commentary on it–which, they say, means either that Wang Pi was suspicious of the chapter or that he did write a commentary but it somehow got mixed in with the text. Also, some scholars have remarked on what they call the "odd style" of the writing. Addressing the first point:

Determining what a long-dead writer thought when he left no written evidence of that seems an exercise in futility. Absence of a commentary could mean anything. It could mean that Wang Pi thought none was needed. It could mean that one got left out in copying. In Chapter Forty-Nine, most of a sentence is missing (see my notes on that chapter) but Wang Pi comments on the sentence, now-missing characters included. In this chapter's case, we have sentences but no commentary. Who knows why? No one.

As for the possibility that a commentary got mixed in with the text:

Wang Pi was born in 226 CE. Two Han Dynasty (206 BCE–220 CE) versions of this chapter, as well as those in the Ma-wang-tui texts, which have been dated to around 200 BCE, are of essentially the same structure as the Wang Pi chapter text, despite differences in individual character choices. Therefore, the Wang Pi text contains no mixed-in commentary.

(The two Ma-wang-tui texts of the *Tao Te Ching*, discovered in 1973, had been written on silk using the "pencil" described in my "Ancient Pictures" introductory section. The silk used for each text had deteriorated considerably by the time of discovery, more so for one text than for the other. The "pencil" had been invented not long before those copies had apparently been made—which, it seems to me, suggests that the copies were most likely written by scribes. The most interesting thing to me about the Ma-wang-tui texts, aside from their placement of what is clearly the second part of the *Tao Te Ching* ahead of what is clearly the first part, is that they show how sloppy the much-criticized scribes of the time, and/or their predecessors, were at copying characters and keeping their hands off the wording of what they were supposed to be duplicating. As literary works, the two texts, which differ from each other in their script types and their character choices, hold together no better than did the silk they were written on.)

Concerning what some scholars have considered the chapter's odd style:

I eliminated five of the *Tao Te Ching*'s eighty-one chapters because of what seemed to be obvious differences from the others in matters such as intelligence, viewpoint, vocabulary, and literary skill. But to me, suspicious though I soon tended to be toward anything in the text that looked at all inconsistent with the rest, this chapter is the author's work at its powerful best. While the style of the chapters I consider authentic can change according to their changing subjects—showing their author's versatility—their intelligence, viewpoint, vocabulary, and literary skill remain consistent. As noted further on, one section of this chapter seemed out-of-place where it was, so I moved it. It had made part of the composition seem scatterbrained—but that was, I believe, someone else's doing. Also, a couple of statements are very sketchy, but that appears to be due to missing characters—a not-uncommon occurrence in the *Tao Te Ching*, a good deal of which is like a once-fine piece of fabric with moth-eaten holes in it.

As for my changes to the chapter's wording:

In the opening sentence, I, like other translators/interpreters, interpreted *ping*, "soldiers," "military," or "weapons," in that stanza's context as "weapons." *Chê*, the character following *ping*—apparently ignored by other interpreters—commonly means "one who," "those who," or "that which." It was originally also used to link parts of a text. So I interpreted it in context as the ancient equivalent of a colon, producing "Man's fine weapons: not good fortune's utensils." In my second stanza's opening sentence, I interpreted *ping* as "soldiers" (other interpreters redundantly use "weapons" again) because of all that follows the sentence, in both that stanza and the remainder of the chapter. Again *chê* followed *ping*, resulting in "Soldiers: not good fortune's utensils." I modified both sentences to make them less abrupt.

In the last line of my first stanza, "live with" is my rewording of "live in," one of the definitions of the text's *ch'u*, "to dwell;" "to live in."

In my second stanza's lines four through eight, I added to the sketchy passage's translation "when such a man," "without them," "he," "may," "but a desire for," and "is his."

The first line of my third stanza is my in-this-context ("princely master," etc.) interpretation of the text's *shêng erh pu mei*, "Conquest thus/then not gentle/peaceful/good." *Mei*, originally composed of "sheep" plus "man," literally meant *gentle man*. The English word I used, *gentleman*, also literally means a *gentle* (well-born, well-bred, thoughtful, considerate) *man*.

The text of lines five through eight of my fourth stanza was located after that of my first stanza. I moved those lines to where they seemed to belong.

The text of my fifth stanza is another sketchy passage, which I translated as "Killed men's multitude accordingly grieve sorrow weeping. Those fought won accordingly funeral rites judge it."

Conquest is not worthy of a gentleman.

Throughout the history of warfare, politicians and military leaders have in one way or another claimed that the purpose of fighting and winning a war is to achieve peace. If that claim were true, our current enormous military expenditures would be buying us an enormous quantity of peace. But they're not, for the easily observable reason that war, like fire, creates more of itself.

Over 2,200 years have passed since the end of the Warring States period. But in all that time, how much progress has been made toward a stable, war-free world?

In the style of the author of the *Sun-tzŭ*, and in the spirit of the author of the *Tao Te Ching*, this author offers here some historically proven principles of warfare:

THE TRUTH OF WAR

An army's business is the winning of wars, not the achieving of peace.

Realistically speaking, no one *wins* a war. A war is "won" when one side ends up losing more than the other.

If two nations fight each other, two nations lose. If three nations fight each other, three nations lose.

A classic warfare saying is: "To the victor belong the spoils." A more accurate saying would be: "To the victor belongs what's been spoiled [by the victor]."

Winning a war produces arrogance. Losing a war produces resentment.

Each war sows the seeds of another. The "holy war" known as the Crusades sowed the seeds that eventually grew into the terrorist attacks on the Pentagon and the World Trade Center, and those that continue today.

The fires of war, when they appear to be quenched, can smolder for generations and then reignite.

One achieves peace through practicing peace. One achieves conflict through practicing conflict.

Inner peace produces outer peace; outer peace produces inner peace. Inner conflict produces outer conflict; outer conflict produces inner conflict. (That can be seen in the "monkey see, monkey do" effect of decades of shoot-out entertainment, a major contributor to the cycle of conflict.)

Warfare benefits the few (military and political leaders, weapons and munitions manufacturers, military contractors) at the expense of the many (everybody else—including the soldiers who have to fight the battles).

No one returns from combat emotionally intact.

In the hearts and minds of those who have fought in a war, that war never ends.

Diplomacy, friendly alliances, and non-aggression agreements achieve much more security for much less cost than military interventions ever can.

Invest the people's money in perpetual preparation for war, and the people will have war and economic hardship. Invest the people's money in perpetual prevention of war, and the people will have peace and prosperity. As the Chinese folk saying puts it, "Sow melons, reap melons. Sow beans, reap beans."

The most dangerous, destructive, and unintelligent war man has ever fought is his relentless war against nature. In that war, everyone will ultimately lose everything.

Peace cannot be made from war any more than water can be made from stone.

32.
WITHOUT TITLES

Here and there in the *Way Virtue Classic*, especially in this chapter, the author seems to be advocating a form of democracy, the opposite of Confucianism, in harmony with the checks and balances of the natural world. Here he is criticizing the tendency of China's governmental systems—in particular, it would appear, the one advocated by the Confucianists—to complicate matters and make people *unequal* to each other.

The character *ming*, used three times in the chapter's text, can mean not only "name," as it's commonly used; it can also mean "title," "designation," "rank," "position," or "fame." In this chapter, "title," "rank," and "position" all seemed appropriate translations. So I used all three, starting with the second line of my first stanza.

In my first stanza, "act" in the tenth line and "behave" in the last line are my in-context interpretations of the text's *tzŭ*, "I," "self," "my," "behavior," "to act." *Tzŭ* is typically interpreted indiscriminately in English-language versions of this and other chapters (such as Chapter Thirty-Seven) as "self."

Chih in the text of my second and third stanzas means "regulation," "a rule," or "a system." I used all three definitions to emphasize the point that the author seems to be making.

Regarding "princes" (first stanza, seventh line): According to one authority, in the time of the feudal kings (which included the Warring States period) *hou* would have meant "prince," while later it would have meant "duke" or "marquis." That would explain why some versions of this and other chapters present *hou* as "prince," while other versions (most that I've seen) present it as "duke" or "marquis."

The Chinese text of my first stanza's lines seven and eight is *hou wang jo nêng shou chih*, "Princes kings if able to guard/to protect/to keep it." Other interpreters of this chapter, Chapter Thirty-Seven, and Chapter Fifty-Two render *shou*, "guard," "protect," or "keep," as "keep" or "hold," or interpret it in words not related to *shou*, such as "keep to," "cling to," "maintain," and so on. But with "keep" as the chosen meaning, the author would seem to be saying in the text of my lines seven through fourteen that "If princes and kings were able to keep it [capture it, lock it up, and keep it for themselves], the ten thousand things would act as their guests. Heaven and earth would notice, and would unite to send sweet dew. The people, without being ordered to do so, would then behave as equals."

It seems more likely that in such a case the ten thousand things would die, heaven and earth would disintegrate, and the people—pretending for the sake of argument that they somehow would survive—would continue in their feudal positions of inequality under the rule of the now-stupendously powerful princes and kings. That is one reason why I chose "guard" and "protect" as the in-context appropriate definitions of *shou*. But I give a better reason next.

Apparently to other interpreters, *shou* as "guard" or "protect" would make no sense. A spirit, most people in Western culture would probably say, cannot be harmed because it is separate from the physical, and therefore to guard or protect a spirit would be meaningless. In contrast, the author indicates in Chapter Sixty that a spirit *can* be harmed, and indicates in Chapter Forty-One, second section, that the spirit he calls The Way is not separate from the physical, *not* separate from its creations.

The following is my explanation of the appropriateness of the interpretation choices "guard" and "protect" in this chapter, Chapter Thirty-Seven, and Chapter Fifty-Two, from this Taoist's point of view:

If someone were to attack you, you would not say to yourself, "He's not attacking *me*, my spiritual self; he's attacking *my body*." Such a distinction would be ridiculous— your assailant would be attacking both your body and the spirit that dwells within it and operates it. Your spirit would know that it is being attacked, and would later remember the attack. It would in truth be harmed by the attack. When we attack the physical world—when we clear-cut forests, put toxic chemicals into the rivers and oceans, and spray poisons on the "weeds" in our yards—we are attacking that world and the spirit within it, the spirit that created it, the spirit that gives us life. We may be too thick-headed and nearsighted to know that, but the spirit knows it. So when we guard and protect the physical world, we guard and protect that spirit, The Mother of the Ten Thousand Things. And it knows it.

If we, like the warring princes and kings mentioned by the author, were to stop attacking The Way of Nature and start protecting her, the ten thousand beings would, as the chapter says, act as our guests—they would esteem and appreciate us instead of fleeing from us as they do now, whenever and however they can.

In my reading of the text, there seemed to be a character missing from the end of the sentence that makes up lines four through six of my second stanza—*ming i chu yu*, "titles/ranks/positions moreover since/sign of the past/past tense have." In my interpretation the last two characters, in this context, mean "since [then] have"—in standard English, "have had." I added "us" after that, as it seemed the most likely possibility to complete the thought.

The typical interpretation of the text of my third stanza goes something like: "The Way's relationship to the world is like that of the great rivers and oceans to the streams and valleys." Translating the characters and filling in where three or possibly more seemed to be missing, I came up with:

[By] comparison[,] Way 's existence heaven under like wide stream [in] deep gorge progressing to large river [progressing to] ocean.

In the text of the above, "wide stream" is *ch'uan*, "a stream formed by the union of other streams." "Deep gorge" is *ku*, "a gorge of great depth." "Large river" is *chiang*, "large river." "Progressing" is one of the ancient meanings of *chih*.

33.
HE WHO . . .

In the text of my first line, the author uses two *chih* characters. The first, literally "arrow-mouth," by dictionary definition means "knowing," "perception," or "wisdom"; the second, literally "arrow-mouth plus sun," means either "knowledge," "cleverness," or "wisdom," depending on context. I interpreted the first *chih* in context as "understands," and the second as "brilliance." For mental brightness, "brilliance" is hard to beat. However:

Ming, the last character in the text of my second line, is made up of "sun" and "moon"—it joins the direct, dazzling light of the sun to the reflected, glowing light of the moon. The fiery sun is *yang*, it burns; the glowing moon is *yin*, it soothes. In terms of human intelligence, the combination could be said to indicate both brilliance and depth, an intelligence that consists of both the logical, problem-solving intellect of *yang* and the deep, introspective wisdom of *yin*. So I interpreted *ming* in this case (and some others, elsewhere) as *enlightenment*.

The last character in the text of my third line is *li*, "muscle," "strength," "energy," "force," typically translated in this chapter as "strength" or "force." But neither of those two definitions provided a contrast with *ch'iang*, "strong," "firm," "determined," the final character of the next line. As *li* pictographically consists of a muscle and its sheath, I chose what seemed the obvious meaning. The author is saying, I believe, that real strength is *more than muscle*.

The text of all but the chapter's final statement consists of paired lines, except for one standalone statement that I interpreted as "He who is content with enough has abundance" (line six). I couldn't resist the temptation to provide it with an accompanying statement, such as it in all probability once had.

In line seven, "moves" is from *hsing*, "to go," "to step." The next character is, again, *ch'iang* ("strong," "firm," "determined"). Not satisfied with "goes strongly," I noticed that another intonation of *ch'iang* means "to force," "to compel." So I rendered *hsing ch'iang* as "moves forcefully." "Resolution" is from *chih*, "will, resolution, fixity of purpose."

In line eight, "endurance" is my in-context version of the text's *chiu*, "long time," "duration." I believe that the preceding characters, *pu shi ch'i so chê*, "not lose his place one who," means "he who stands his ground."

A book I read years ago claimed that the Asian Studies terrain is littered with the bones of those who were foolhardy enough to attempt to translate, interpret, and understand the *Tao Te Ching*. This chapter's last statement appeared to be one of the many reasons why. The characters seemed to be saying that "he who dies but does not die has longevity." But how can someone die but not die? And how can someone who dies have *longevity*? The typical interpretation starts with something like: "He who dies but does not perish."

I looked for a workable alternative to "dies" in the definitions of the statement's first "death" character, *ssu*, but found only "to die," "death," "firm," and "obstinate." *Wang*, the second "death" character, proved a different case. Although *wang* is defined in its more modern, brush-written form as "to die, perish, cease to exist," its ancient ancestor depicted someone *entering a hiding place*, and was defined as "to disappear," "lost," "absent," "gone away," "passed away." From the ancient definitions, I concluded that the author means that someone who dies but does not disappear from other people's awareness "lives" in their memories for a long time.

34.
THE GREAT WAY

Like The Great Way in the first line, the interpretation of this chapter just seemed to *flow*. The chapter turned out to be one of the few I'd by then encountered in the *Way Virtue Classic* that did not seem to have something significant missing or something insignificant added. I therefore was able to use all of the characters, except for an exclamation/emphasis character and an emphasis/interrogative, neither of which worked well in English. It was a great pleasure to work on such an unspoiled chapter.

Fan, which I interpreted as "flows everywhere" (first stanza, first line), is defined as "inundate," "vast." It consists of *shui*, "water," plus *han*, "to blossom," "to expand."

Kuei has two meanings appropriate to the chapter's context: "to return" and "to belong to." Undecided about which would be better to use, I used both (first stanza, next-to-last sentence).

As a former Bible-studies student, I would say that the wording of this chapter, whether in Chinese or in faithful-to-the-characters English, resembles the powerful writing style of Isaiah—but from a *yin*-favoring viewpoint.

The theme that flows through the *Way Virtue Classic* as a river flows through a landscape is that the *yin* is greater than the *yang*—what small minds consider the inferior of the two earthly energies is for many reasons the superior. As for the greatest earthly *yin* power, The Mother of the Ten Thousand Things, "The ten thousand things rely on it, and flourish, and do not refuse it. It accomplishes deeds of excellence, yet does not have a title—it clothes and feeds the ten thousand things and does not act their lord. . . . Because it ultimately does not conduct itself as great, it is therefore able to achieve its greatness." Proceeding not with pushy arrogance but with yielding modesty, it meets no resistance. Meeting no resistance, it is able to overcome and effortlessly rule.

It seems to me that one reason why the author had such strong contempt for Confucianism is that it was a *yang* philosophy, a "lord and master" political philosophy that allocated the greatest honor and power to those at the top of the social/governmental pyramid (while encouraging them to behave themselves), from whom help for those below them was supposed to descend, along the lines of trickle-down economics. But human nature is what it is: Those who have power and wealth want more, not less. And they want to hold on to what they have, not share it. Unfortunately for the majority, the Confucian hierarchy-rules locked everyone in place. The only escape for the disadvantaged came later, with the advent of grueling civil-service examinations that at least in theory enabled any man—but no woman—from a lower-income family to compete for one of the relatively small number of available government jobs.

As for the born-*yin* half of the Chinese population: Women of the author's time simply had no rights. As Confucianism gained power in the succeeding centuries, women would be increasingly restricted, remaining increasingly unheard and unseen—shut away "behind the screen," as the Chinese saying puts it. (Doctors, for example, could only diagnose a woman's ailments by taking the pulse of a hand extended from behind a screen.)

The author had most likely seen all around him what the "lord and master," "top gorilla" mentality tended to lead to: fighting, fighting, and more fighting. The results of that behavior-tendency, left unchecked, were *stress* and *destruction*. The author's alternative was based on the *yin* behavior of The Way of Nature, The Valley Spirit, which operates with a light touch—the opposite of the heavy-handed "lord and master" approach that every government of China, including the present one, has to one degree or another practiced.

When the author wrote of the power of *yin*, he was ahead of his time. Today, around 2,400 years later, he's ahead of our time as well.

35.

THE IMAGE OF NOTIIINGNESS

The following is my generic version of other interpretations I've read of Chapter Thirty-Five:

"If you hold to the Great Image, the world will come to you—will come to you without injury and find safety, peace, and quiet. Music and food will cause passersby to stop; but a description of The Way has no taste, no flavor. Looked at, it cannot be seen; listened to, it cannot be heard—but when it is used, it cannot be exhausted."

There are some problems with such interpretations of what's being said. First, although they flesh out the character-meanings with words in order to make them say this or that, they add no words to specify to readers what the "Great Image" is or may be, or to explain why visitors will not be (or would be expected to be) injured. Second, why will the world come to you if you hold to the Great Image? Third, if those mentioned passersby drop in because they hear music and smell food, what satisfaction will they gain from something that has no flavor and that can't be seen or heard? Fourth, why would they or anyone else then use it—because there's so much of it that it can't be used up? And, fifth point, the characters don't say what they've been manipulated to say. Mostly they say the opposite.

To those accustomed to "Western" (Middle Eastern) spiritual teachings, the statement "If you hold to the Great Image, the world will come to you" may seem appealing—such would be a verification of one's spirit power, charisma, or "star quality."

To Taoists, however, such a concept is frightening. And, as I'll explain a bit further on, the characters of the text don't translate as "come to you."

But first, here are some words—the relevance of which will soon be apparent—about a very significant influence on *Tao Te Ching* interpretation:

Born in 226 CE, the brilliant scholar and philosopher Wang Pi ("wahng bee") wrote commentaries, highly regarded to this day, on the *Tao Te Ching* and the *I Ching* ("yee jeeng"), the *Changes Classic*. His *I Ching* commentary presented that work as a book of wisdom rather than as the manual of divination that it was then exclusively considered to be, thereby placing it on the firm foundation of reason. His commentary on the *Tao Te Ching* maintained that The Way is equivalent to *wu*, "emptiness" or "nothingness," which is deeper than the *t'ai chi*, the two powers of *yin* and *yang*, The Dark and The Light. Its point of view opposed and eventually superseded the one then prevalent, the dominance of which had been largely due to the *yin yang chia*, the "Yin Yang School," which had begun late in the Warring States period. In going up against the *yin yang chia*, Wang Pi returned public attention to the *Tao Te Ching*'s apparently original term, *wu chi*, "Highest Nothingness."

Aside from the matter of his commentary, the very old text of the *Tao Te Ching* that he chose to remark on is still considered the most authoritative and reliable—the clearest, most sensible, most articulate, and most literary of all.

Wang Pi's death in 249 CE at the age of twenty-three deprived the world of one of the finest minds in the history of philosophy.

That having been said, there is another side to Wang Pi's *Tao Te Ching* commentary:

Wang Pi belonged to the *hsüan-hsüeh* ("Mystery-Learning") movement, known in the West as "neo-Taoism"—a movement that joined Taoist ideas to Confucian principles. Significantly, the *hsüan-hsüeh* considered Master K'ung to have been more enlightened than either Master Lao or Master Chuang (Chuang Chou), Taoism's second-most-important writer—a rather odd stance, considering that Master K'ung stayed well away from the metaphysical. Among the *hsüan-hsüeh* beliefs was that one must abandon likes and dislikes (no more criticism of Confucianism and rulers) and therefore ignore the outer world and focus on the inner—a point of view far more related to the philosophy of Master Chuang than to that of the *Tao Te Ching*'s author.

In my opinion, Wang Pi's brilliance actually worked *against* an understanding of the *Tao Te Ching*. It reached its conclusions too quickly; it ran swiftly over details that it should have paid more attention to—such as the vitally important original meanings of characters. Wang Pi's commentary bent too many of the brush-character meanings in order to suit his personal and *hsüan-hsüeh* beliefs. (Interpreting a passage by "bending" meanings is rather like forcing a jigsaw-puzzle piece into a space not made for it, instead of searching for a piece that fits—a form of winning by cheating.) And his legendarily flamboyant, argumentative, "showman" tendencies were, in my opinion, ill-suited for exploring the depth and breadth of the enigmatic-in-its-simplicity *Tao Te Ching*.

As an example of why I consider Wang Pi's commentary to have been a "mixed bag": Its interpretation of Chapter One's opening statement was based on Wang Pi's stated belief that "wayed" in "way can be wayed" meant *identified and described* as a way—as he put it, "pointed to" and "reproduced [in words]" as a way—rather than simply and directly meaning *done* (followed, traveled on, emulated) as a way. Words, wrote Wang Pi, cannot reveal *the constant nature* of whatever they are being used to describe—therefore, "way can be wayed [told about] *not* Constant [and, therefore, *not* Eternal] Way." Had he taken a more careful and objective look at the *entire* chapter, as well as at the "*being* versus *non-being*" theme of various other chapters, he might have seen that the opening chapter's opening statement was simply introducing what the author later refers to as The Valley Spirit and The Way of Heaven. Then his commentary could have been quite different from the convoluted and confusing razzle-dazzle translated and briefly quoted from here.

> A thing that exists originates in nothingness. Therefore, before it has form, and is still without name, [The Way] operates as the origin of the ten thousand things. Once it has form and has name, it produces them, rears them, gives each its proper shape, and brings them to maturity as their mother. In other words, The Way by itself being without form and without name, originates the ten thousand things and brings them to completion. They are begun and finished in this manner, yet know not how that happens. That is the "darkness upon darkness."

Wang Pi's "way that can be described" interpretation strongly influenced the earliest Western interpreters—Jesuits and Protestant missionaries who added their own doctrine-based assumptions about what the author was saying throughout the *Way Virtue Classic*. The combination continues to influence and intimidate *Tao Te Ching* interpreters today.

Regarding my interpretation of Chapter Thirty-Five:

In my first stanza, I added the second line (borrowed from Chapter Fourteen) to indicate what the "great image" is: the image of *Nothingness* (*wu wu chih hsiang*, "without-thing's image"). The Way of Heaven is invisible. In Taoism, there is no equivalent of Michelangelo's image of God on the Sistine Chapel ceiling, an image created in the image of man. The image of Nothingness is akin to that of The Void in Buddhism. One "holds to" it by *feeling*.

Concerning "wanders by" in my first stanza's third line, my interpretation of the character *wang*: *Wang* consists of the "radical" (root character) *ch'ih*, "to step with the left foot," signifying *stepping out*, joined by the "phonetic" (sound-giving character) *wang*, which depicts tufts of vegetation growing here and there, and which in ancient times signified *rambling, wandering*. Originally the compound character *wang* meant "to stray," "to roam about," "to wander away." It signified *aimlessness*. The more modern, brush-written character evolved into meaning "start," "go toward" (not "come to," as previous interpretations of this chapter have it), and also "pass, go past" and "past." So the "the world will come to you" interpretation contradicts the definitions of the brush-written character as well as those of its ancestor.

In the fourth line of my first stanza, "disturb" is my version of *hai*, "injure" (the context: *pu hai an p'ing t'ai*, "not injure peace harmony supreme").

In the second stanza, I added "elsewhere" (first line) and "may make" (third line) to prevent any perceived inconsistency with the message of the first stanza's text—that wanderers will not stop to visit.

The following is my translation of the text of my second stanza's lines four through ten, including its exclamation/emphasis character. Its "description" is from *ch'u k'ou*, "[what] comes out [of] mouth."

> [But The] Way's description [is] tasteless! It [is] without flavor. Look—it [is] not enough to see. Listen—it [is] not enough to hear.

Unlike the authors of most English-language versions I've seen of this chapter, I decided that "it" (*ch'i*) in the above is *The Way*, not *a description of* The Way. So I substituted "The Way" for the first "it." If one interprets that "it" as meaning *a description of* The Way, line six is redundant and the lines after that are nonsensical.

The stanza's final sentence, "When one makes use of it, there is not enough to satiate," is from the text's *yung chih pu tsu chi*, "Use [it]—it [is] not enough to finish/all/ done." The last character, *chi* ("to finish," "all," "done"), pictographically means *to belch after the meal*—to reach satiation. (An explanation: The Way, being elusive, mysterious, and insubstantial, does not completely satisfy its followers' hunger for its wisdom and spirit-power, in order to help them learn step by step how to develop their own.)

I started these notes on the chapter by summing up other interpretations I've read of it. Now I'll sum up mine:

The author is saying—humorously, I think—that when one holds to the image of No-Image, that of The Way of Heaven, one has nothing that would interest strangers passing by. But from that flavorless, invisible, inaudible, non-satiating Way, one has *an p'ing t'ai* (the text of my first stanza's last line)—supreme peace and harmony.

36.
DELETED

I eliminated the hodgepodge traditionally known as the thirty-sixth chapter for the following reasons:

(1) The first section of the alleged chapter consists of four very questionable assertions, such as "[If you] will want [to] weaken it, [you] must certainly strengthen it," followed by a questionable claim: "This [is] called 'hidden brightness.'" *Very* hidden, I think. "It" in each assertion is not identified. ("It" = "something"?)

(2) The second section consists of a sentence paraphrased from Chapter Seventy-Eight: "The soft and weak conquer the hard and strong."

(3) The third section consists of two more questionable assertions: "Fish [are] not able to escape from whirling water at the bottom of an abyss" (the last eight words are the ancient meaning of *yüan*, now meaning simply "abyss"): and "[A] nation's sharp/clever/profitable utensils/tools [are] not able accordingly [to be] revealed [to] people." (*I i,* "sharp/clever/profitable," consists of the character for "growing grain" joined to that for "knife," the combination of which means *scythe* or *mowing tool*—"grain knife"—which therefore means *sharp, clever,* or *profitable*.) No English-language *Tao Te Ching* that I've seen presents these strange statements according to what their characters are actually saying. Instead:

The well-known and often-quoted "translations" of the two assertions are: "Fish should not leave deep water" and "A nation's sharpest weapons should not be shown to the people."

37.
TRANQUILITY

Most of the presentations I've seen of Chapter Thirty-Seven start out with one version or another of: "The Way is constantly without doing, yet nothing is not done. If marquises and kings could keep it, the ten thousand things would transform themselves. Once they were transformed, if their desires would arise, I would subdue them with the nameless simplicity [*What* is *that*?]. With the nameless simplicity, men also would be without desires. Having no desires would produce tranquility, and under heaven would quiet itself."

Dissatisfied for various reasons with all of the interpretations I'd seen, I eventually arrived at one that made a good deal more sense to me. To summarize what I came to believe the author is saying: The Way operates and accomplishes without *striving*, and yet without *not-acting*. If rulers were able to protect it, all of the natural world (which operates effortlessly, in alliance with The Way) would transform them, making them better, happier people. If the rulers then found that some of their old desires (to conquer, destroy, and dominate) were still in place, their improved awareness would overcome those desires with the Natural Simplicity (*p'u*) of "Without-Name" (*wu ming*), The Way. The Way's operating simplicity, which does what needs to be done *and no more*, would then be used by all of the rulers' subjects: "Men also [meaning not just the rulers now, but everyone] would be without desires, not-desiring with tranquility. All under heaven would behave peacefully."

My final interpretation was the result of two courses of action:

First, although I followed the characters—with the exception of one noted further on—I ended up interpreting six of them differently from the traditional way.

The first three are in the chapter's opening sentence, *tao ch'ang wu wei erh wu pu wei*, traditionally presented as "The Way is constantly without doing, yet nothing is not done." I wasn't satisfied with *wu* ("without, absence of" or "non-being, nothingness") as "nothing" the second time it appears in that first sentence. Nor was I satisfied with "The Way is constantly without doing." The Way is constantly *doing*, I thought, or nothing in nature would get done. But The Way does not *strive* or *force*, which are two of the most common ways that the author uses *wei* (classical definitions: "do," "act," "cause," etc.) throughout the *Tao Te Ching*. So I translated the statement as "[The] Way [is] constantly without doing, yet without not-doing," which I then interpreted as (with emphasis here on my three interpretation differences) "The Way is constantly without [*wu*] striving [*wei*], and yet *without* [*wu*] *not-acting [pu wei].*"

The fourth of the six character-interpretation differences was of *shou* "guard," "protect," "keep," which I interpreted as "guard" and "protect" in my fifth line, as I had in Chapter Thirty-Two for reasons given in that chapter's notes.

The fifth character-interpretation difference was of *tzŭ*, "self," "I," "my own," "personally," "behavior," "to act, action," traditionally interpreted throughout the *Tao Te Ching* as "self." I interpreted it as "act" (seventh line) and as "behave" (next-to-last line), as I'd done in Chapter Thirty-Two.

The sixth character-interpretation difference was of hua, "to change," "to transform," "to improve," "to civilize," which in my seventh line I interpreted as "to improve." Which resulted in "act to improve" (*tzŭ hua*), rather than the usual interpretation's "self-transform." There seemed to be a character missing after *tzŭ hua*, "act to improve," so I added "them." (Possibly a copyist, having understood *tzŭ hua* to mean "self-transform," had eliminated as an error a character following those two.) I'd started out in the traditional way, translating *tzŭ hua* as "self-transform," but that had made the lines after seem nonsensical—they'd then said that the Way-favoring actions of the princes and kings would cause the ten thousand things to transform *themselves*, but that they, the ten thousand things, might have remaining desires. As the author tells us in other chapters, however, the ten thousand things, like the wise who emulate them, *do not have* desires. (The wise have *spiritual* desires, as indicated in Chapter One, but not *greed-feeding* ones.) And why would the Way-favoring actions of the rulers cause the ten thousand things to transform *themselves*? *They* aren't the ones causing trouble. And what would they be, and what good would they be, transformed?

My second course of action—the above interpretation differences being the first—was to change *wu*, "I," in the text of my tenth line to another *wu*. When I at first trustingly used *wu*, "I," I translated the third sentence as: "[If they were] improved, but [still] desiring [to] act, I would restrain them by means of Without-Name's Natural Simplicity." But how could the author restrain the desires of princes, kings, or anyone else? Why would he believe that he could do so—megalomania? So I went looking for other *wu* characters, thinking that someone must have written the wrong one, and immediately spotted *wu*, "awaken," "discern," "comprehend," "consciousness," "intelligence." This *wu* consists of the above character for "I," *wu*, joined by a simplified version of that for "mind" or "heart," *hsin*. I came to the obvious conclusion: The copyist didn't complete the character.

Finally, I changed my character-by-character translation's "[If they were] improved, but [still] desiring [to] act" to: "Improved, if they still desired to take aggressive action" (lines eight and nine), in order to make clearer what I believe the author is saying.

38.
VIRTUE AND PROPRIETY

This chapter might appropriately be titled "Having Fun with Confucianism." But before getting started on that:

To help clarify what *te*, "Virtue," is—which is more than what our word "virtue" would indicate—I'm including the following description by the classical scholar and *Tao Te Ching* specialist Yen-ling Feng, translated by Red Pine in his book *Lao-tzu's Taoteching*:

> Virtue is the manifestation of the Way. The Way is what Virtue contains. Without the way, Virtue would have no power. Without Virtue, the Way would have no appearance.

One could therefore say that *te*, "Virtue," is the power and character of The Way as manifested by some human beings, as well as by the ten thousand things.

The text of my first stanza, translated, reads: "High Virtue not Virtue; therefore has Virtue. Low Virtue not lose Virtue; therefore without Virtue." In case the meaning of those playing-with-characters statements is unclear, and in case the author's next remarks don't make it clearer:

High Virtue does not focus on or work at what is defined and talked about as "Virtue." It lives Virtue effortlessly, without even being aware of it, going above and beyond the norm. It does not display "Virtue." Therefore, it has Virtue. (Many people will not see it, though, because they look for "Virtue.") Low Virtue focuses on and works at what is defined and talked about as "Virtue." Having worked to attain it, it makes sure that it does not lose it. It is very aware of what it's got. It displays "Virtue" in its conduct. Therefore, it does not have Virtue. To put it simply, Low Virtue works hard at proving what High Virtue doesn't have to prove and what it doesn't care about proving. (Also: see Chapter Twenty-One's first statement.)

In the text of my second stanza, the author tells what he thinks of the Confucian principles *jên* (Benevolence), *i* (Righteousness), and *li* (Propriety): High Benevolence is on the same level as Virtue, but doesn't know it; High Righteousness is below it; and as for High Propriety:

Regarding the author's remark about stuffy High Propriety's angry response to Virtue's response, I didn't misread those characters—they're very clear:

high propriety strives [for] it [virtue] and negatively it
responds consequently [high propriety] seizes [its] arm
and flings away it

Other interpretations of the last five characters say things about men rolling up their sleeves or baring their arms.

The author obviously has no liking for Propriety's artificial system of hierarchy rules and antiquity-imitating rituals, which were to be followed exactly and without exception. There's a famous saying about Master K'ung: "If the mat was not straight, the Master would not sit." That's Propriety.

In the text of my fourth stanza, the author mentions two more Confucian principles, *chung* (Loyalty) and *hsin* (Sincerity), saying in effect that the man of Propriety (the man of *rules* and *form*) doesn't honor his alleged accompanying principles of Loyalty and Sincerity, and thereby brings about confusion.

He goes on to say that, because Propriety sets rigid rules for dealing with incidents and situations that haven't yet occurred and that therefore can't presently be predicted or understood, the man of Propriety—*ch'ien shih chê*, "one who advance-knows," says the text—is "stupidity's beginning." The eventual downfall of increasingly inflexible Confucianist China testifies to the truth of that assertion.

In the fourth stanza's sixth line, I added "by the rules of Propriety" for clarity.

39.

THESE ACQUIRED THE ONE
TAKING THE LOWLY AS THE ROOT

In the next-to-last line of my first section's first stanza, "fortunate" is my interpretation of *chên*, "inquire by divination," "auspicious," "good, virtuous," "firm, solid." The character consists of "divination" plus "money."

In the second stanza, "dispersing" (line two) is my interpretation of *lieh*, now defined as "crack, split, rip open." The original character depicted a river that had overflowed its banks and cut new channels through the fields, joined to the character for "clothes"—the combination meaning "the scattered remnants of cloth left after a garment is cut out," or simply "scatter."

In the fourth line of the second stanza, "erupting" is my interpretation of *fa*, the many meanings of which include "rise," "expand," "launch, send out," "issue." The character shows a bow launching an arrow.

In my second section, the author appears to be advising members of the nobility that if they wish to gain more support from the people they rule, they would be wise to incorporate more humble, of-the-people *yin* into their behavior, and less haughty, aggressively aristocratic *yang*. Consequently, in the first stanza, I added "gaining through modesty" (line six).

In ancient China, *shu yü*, "many carriages," was a way of saying *noble* or *wealthy*—carriages then being, like today's fine automobiles, status symbols. The text of the first two lines of my second section's second stanza is *chih shu yü wu yü*, "Make many-carriages absence-of-carriages."

Regarding the chapter's two final lines: An ancient Chinese saying maintains that "One can recognize an aristocrat in passing by the tinkling sound of jade."

40.

RETURNING

"Return" (*fan*, the chapter's first character) is an important principle of Taoism. Everything in nature moves in cycles, returning: Water flows downward, returning to the sea, from which it rises as vapor and returns, falling on the land; animal life and plant life return to the soil; seasons leave and return; so do darkness and light. Everything comes from The Way; everything returns to it. The wise return to childlike simplicity, sincerity, and clear vision. The Taoist meditator "returns to The Source."

The text of my second line is generally interpreted as "Weakness is the useful-ness of the Way," or something similar. I interpreted *jo*, "weak" or "weakness," "tender" or "tenderness," as *tenderness*. And I interpreted *yung*, "use" or "usage," "employ" or "employment," as *utilization*.

41.

HEARING OF THE WAY
THE WAY IS HIDDEN

Readers familiar with the *Tao Te Ching* may wonder what happened to the lengthy passage between what I made into the chapter's two sections—the passage that in the typical translation starts "Therefore, it is said" (literally "Therefore, established words have it") and goes on (and on) about the bright path being like darkness, the advancing path being like retreat, the great square having no corners, and so on.

Having re-read the passage several times, I asked myself three questions: First, why does the author, instead of making his point in his usual waste-no-words manner, expend so much effort on redundancy, providing illustration after illustration of one simple, easy-to-grasp idea? Second, why does he turn hyper-cerebral on us, and more than a bit surreal? Third, why do those supposedly traditional sayings ("established words") read suspiciously like statements made by writers of the School of Names?

The School of Names, which came into existence in the Warring States period, concerned itself in a very intellectual, hair-splitting way with the relationship of "names" (words) to reality. One philosopher of the School of Names was Kung-sun Lung, famous for very cleverly proving that "A white horse is not a horse"—a revelation that must have been startling to white horses everywhere. Another member of the school was Hui Shih, known for declarations such as "Heaven and earth are equally low; mountains and marshes are equally level" and "The sun at noon is setting; when an animal is born, it dies." Hui Shih is the "Hui-tzŭ" mentioned in the writings of Master Chuang.

Of course, I could be wrong. The parade of paradoxes could have been contrived by the *Tao Te Ching*'s author in an uncharacteristically long-winded, hyper-intellectual, and showoff mood. But I doubt it.

In my first section, lines six and seven ("At first seems to retain it / Then seems to lose it") are from *jo ts'un jo wang*, "resembles/as if preserve/keep/store resembles/as if lose/escape/disappear [ancient meanings of *wang*, now defined as "die," "cease"]."

I added "If it were" (line eleven), "by such men" (line twelve), and "it would" (line thirteen).

Below are what seemed the most-likely relevant definitions of the seven characters that make up the text of my second section's concluding statement. I believe that the redundant third character was someone's addition, and that there is a character, or maybe two, missing after the fifth one.

(1) The one in question; (2) only; (3) Way; (4) good/kind/virtuous; (5) loan/lend; (6) meanwhile/however; (7) perfect/whole/complete.

I interpreted the above as: "Only that Nameless One kindly lends itself to all while, however, remaining perfectly whole, complete." The usual interpretation goes something like: "The Way alone gives life to all things and brings them to completion." The first part of that interpretation seemed so obvious and so frequently previously stated and implied that it hardly needed to be said yet again. The second part bothered me because—despite what Wang Pi says in his various chapter-commentaries—by no means are all things brought to completion. I didn't think that sort of interpretation was as in line with the author's intelligence, or as deep as, and therefore as likely as, the higher-viewpoint idea of The Way lending its energy to everything and everyone, yet not diminishing itself—especially since the latter interpretation, unlike others I'd seen, follows the characters. Going by those characters, what else could the author possibly mean? The key to what he's saying is the seemingly overlooked-by-others phrase *shan* ("good," "kind," "virtuous") *tai* ("loan, lend").

Only that Nameless One kindly lends itself to all.

The Way lends itself to everything in nature, and therefore is found in everything in nature. But nowhere can its presence be more easily recognized than in the life-giver known as *water*.

Water, say Taoists from the author of the *Tao Te Ching* on down, is a great teacher—*the* great teacher. For thousands of years, its behavior has been observed and emulated by the wise. That great teacher and life force, say Taoists, deserves appreciation and respect. Yet what it has long received from the human race has been mostly *poisons* and *neglect*.

Sampled stream, river, lake, and tap water has by now been found to contain every toxic metal tested for—lead, mercury, copper, selenium, zinc, cadmium, and arsenic—as well as nearly seven hundred deadly chemical compounds, including dioxins, polychlorinated biphenyls (PCBs), hydrocarbons, plasticizers, flame retardants, and a variety of dangerous-side-effects pharmaceuticals.

Regarding arsenic: The United States is the world's leading user, typically in the areas of industrialized (corporate) farming and suburban home-and-business lawn care, in which are applied fertilizers containing weed killer—arsenic—the presence of which can easily be detected by its bitter smell. As a result, arsenic is increasingly being found in our foods, especially in grapes, wine, and non-organic rice and rice products.

From large-scale corporate farming operations also come pesticides, herbicides, hormones, and antibiotics. Glyphosate, used in more than seven hundred weed killers and recently shown to cause cancer, has been found in all human urine tested, including that of babies. Glyphosate is known as a xenoestrogen, an estrogen mimic powerful enough to fool the human body into reacting to it as to the natural hormone. Xenoestrogens are found in many plastics, detergents, deodorants, body lotions, building materials, and electronics, as well as in genetically modified (GMO) foods. They throw human hormones out of balance, cause human bodies to store fat—which triggers increased estrogen production in both men and women, which in turn triggers more storage of fat—and cause serious male problems, including reduced muscle mass and strength and increased fatigue and depression. So much estrogen/xenoestrogen is in water now that it's causing male fish and frogs to become females. Researchers recently discovered that 40 percent of the male bass captured in the Potomac River for one study were producing eggs.

Also found in drinking water are nitrates and phosphates from large-scale farms, animal feedlots, and suburban lawn care. Their runoff is creating oxygen-starved dead zones in areas off our coasts, in which no marine life can exist.

Studies of women exposed to half the amount of nitrogen (used in chemical fertilizers) considered safe by federal standards have revealed an increased risk of bladder, ovarian, and thyroid cancers. One such study has revealed higher-than-normal rates of birth defects.

In a recent three-ocean study of seven species of sea turtles, pieces of plastic were found in the stomach of every turtle examined. In the stomachs of sea turtles have also been found rubber bands and pieces of balloons. Recently in Indonesia, a dead whale washed ashore had in its stomach 115 plastic cups, four plastic bottles, twenty-five plastic bags, two flip-flop sandals, a nylon sack, and more than one thousand other assorted pieces of plastic. Recently in Oregon, the stomach of a rescued sickly sea turtle was found to be completely filled with plastic. Ultra-fine microplastic particles have recently been discovered in our drinking water.

The equivalent of one truckload of plastic is said to enter the ocean every minute. The production of throwaway plastic is expected to quadruple by 2050. Chemicals from today's plastics will contaminate our water, food, and bodies for decades. And the undersea world will continue to die.

Water has *memory*—it retains something of what is put into it. As a result of centuries of human contamination and neglect, it is low in oxygen and electron energy, both of which can be only partially restored by nature through rapid water flow and churning—as in waterfall and ocean-wave action—and neither of which can be fully restored by known filtration and purification processes. Our planet's water is *tired*, like someone exposed to extraordinary stresses for too long a period of time.

Ecologically, water's amazing ability to *receive* and *retain* is considered its weakness, as it is therefore greatly susceptible to toxins. But, as with all *yin* energy, within its "weakness" can be found its strength. The following paragraphs give some examples of that principle in action:

Water's extraordinary ability to absorb whatever has been given to it has been documented by Doctor of Alternative Medicine Masaru Emoto. Dr. Emoto studied micro-cluster water and magnetic resonance analysis technology, and carried out extensive research into water worldwide. His book *The Hidden Messages in Water* (Beyond Words Publishing, Hillsboro, Oregon, 2004) became a *New York Times* best seller.

Dr. Emoto captured images of frozen water crystals ("snowflakes") using high-speed photography. He discovered by experimentation that water from clear springs, when exposed to positive thoughts, positive words, or classical music, formed brilliant and complex snowflake patterns, while clear water exposed to negative thoughts, negative words, or heavy metal music formed asymmetrical or incomplete patterns and repellant colors, like those formed from the polluted water he tested.

The Hidden Messages in Water contains many color photographs of those crystals. In one experiment, a sample of clear water was intentionally ignored in favor of other water samples. Its photograph shows only a vague beginning of a crystal pattern. The most beautiful and best-formed crystals shown are those created in response to verbal expressions of love and gratitude and the words "Wisdom" and "You're beautiful." A photograph of an ugly, malformed, brown crystal made from lake water is contrasted with that of a pale violet, perfectly formed crystal from the same water after a Buddhist healing prayer was spoken to it. Photographs of crystals made from distilled water heated in microwave ovens, exposed to mobile-phone energy, or placed next to computers show distorted, sick-looking forms.

In a large-scale experiment, Dr. Emoto asked a Shinto priest to repeat one of the nature-honoring Japanese religion's incantations for an hour at the edge of the lake formed by Fujiwara Dam in central Japan while he videotaped the event. His research team collected samples of water from the lake before and after the chanting. Within fifteen minutes after the incantation had ended, the murky water had begun to clear and those present could see vegetation at the lake bottom. According to Dr. Emoto, crystals formed from the samples taken before the chanting had begun were "distorted . . . like the face of someone in great pain," while those formed from the water taken after the incantation were "complete and grand."

Until relatively recently, the only spiritual teachings in America that have strongly acknowledged, taught of, and emphasized daily harmony with the presence of divine spirit everywhere in nature have been those of the surviving nations (tribes) of the Original Americans, the "Indians." (They wouldn't be known as Indians today if not for Christopher Columbus's mistake. They would likely be known as what they are—Americans.)

So how have those appreciators of and collaborators with the spirit within nature been treated from the beginning of this nation by followers of the newer-arrival religious denominations who said (but not demonstrated) that they believed in the presence of divine spirit in everything?

As the newcomers spread westward, slaughtering buffalo and "Indians" in the process, some of the foreign-religion followers endeavored to teach the proclaimed savages the error of their ways—their Native American ways—by founding and operating schools in which they beat, shamed, and otherwise bullied and intimidated their charges into accepting and exclusively practicing *their* religion, that of (ironically) "the Prince of Peace" (whose recorded compassion for the persecuted doesn't seem to have rubbed off on them).

It's unfortunate that the teachers did not respect, listen to, or learn from those on whom they were forcing their religion. If they had done so, today's American landscape might have been a far more unspoiled one—something bearing a much-closer resemblance to the paradise it once was. And the constant appreciators of the one Great Spirit present in nature would not have been what they were in this nation's past and what they are in its present—the most persecuted but otherwise neglected people in the United States of America.

The Indian Removal Act of 1830 legalized the forceful removal of Original Americans from their long-cherished homelands to areas far from them, and far from the newcomers' civilization. As that civilization expanded westward, its government moved those Americans again and again to increasingly desolate areas. More than five hundred land-granting treaties were written, signed, and then broken by the dishonest and disrespectful government.

Today the "reservations"—detention centers with invisible walls—have shrunk to 2.3 percent of the land area first promised. They are typically located in arid places unsuitable for agriculture and far from towns, making the growing of crops and the transportation to the reservations of real food with short shelf-lives (as distinguished from the lifeless junk and sugary soda pop found in the usual reservation store) troublesome, expensive, and unprofitable.

Because reservation unemployment rates can reach 85 percent, parents frequently must move to job locations in faraway towns, leaving their children to be brought up by grandparents and causing family life to be broken up. Basic services such as healthcare, schools, and stores are often an hour's drive or more away, so money that could have been spent on quality food for the children is often spent on gasoline for the long trips by car. Because affordable nutritious food is scarce, Original Americans are far more likely than other Americans to die of afflictions such as diabetes, cancer, and tuberculosis. Their health also suffers from eco-degradation originating elsewhere but affecting the reservations—such as groundwater contamination, illegal dumping and hazardous waste disposal, air pollution, mining-waste toxicity, and habitat destruction.

The Original American population is the poorest in the Northern Hemisphere, surviving (barely) in third-world conditions. The typical reservation's poverty is extreme, its residents living in run-down houses and trailers, many of which have no electricity, telephone, running water, or sewage system.

The U.S. Supreme Court ruled in 1908 that the tribes are entitled to sufficient water to make their reservations livable homelands. But in many states, the government has instead provided huge subsidies for *non*-Indians to develop water access and use it for themselves, causing reservation wells (many over one thousand feet deep) to run short of water—while doing little or nothing to provide reservation access to clean and adequate water. In the increasingly heating-up, drought-prone Southwest, reservation residents, often including children and grandparents equipped only with buckets for water collecting, need to travel long distances to the wells that are still working.

Original Americans are more frequently stopped by police for questioning than are members of any other racial or ethnic group. More of them are killed by police than are members of any other racial or ethnic group. No one knows how many Original American women are murdered or go missing every year, because missing persons statistics—which are compiled for all other racial and ethnic groups—are not compiled for them. Among Original Americans, depression and suicides are epidemic. Native teenagers are three times more likely to commit suicide than are other adolescents.

Original American students account for only 1 percent of American college students. They are rarely treated well by classmates and professors, and frequently leave school because of that.

As an Indian-activist friend once remarked to me, "American Indians, unlike other minorities, don't complain—so their predicament is ignored. American Indians have the warrior mindset. Warriors don't *complain*—they just *die*."

Few people seem to know how much this nation owes to North America's oldest democracy—that established in around 1150 CE by the Great Law of Peace, the creation of the five-nation Iroquois League, which in 1722 expanded into the Six Nation Iroquois Confederacy. Under the Great Law, each member nation had a voice in the governing of the whole; each village and clan had a representative at the internation council; each member of the five-then-six nations had equal voting rights; men and women shared power. The Great Law inspired Thomas Jefferson, Alexander Hamilton, and "the Father of the Constitution," James Madison (to whom this writer happens to be related), as they and others worked out the structure of the United States government and the wording of its Constitution. The Iroquois Confederacy's Grand Council of Chiefs inspired the creation of the U.S. Congress. The elected presiding Chief of Chiefs inspired the creation of an elected U.S. president. And the Clan Mothers, who served for life and who had the power to appoint or remove chiefs, inspired the creation of the U.S. Supreme

Court. That three-branch structure served as the model for the three branches of our government—the legislative, the executive, and the judicial.

Even the official seal of our new nation of thirteen states and strong central government was inspired by Iroquois precedent: It featured an eagle clutching thirteen arrows (representing the original states), adapted from the Iroquois League's cluster of five arrows (representing the original five nations), which symbolized *strength through unity*.

That was in our nation's beginning. As for its present and future:

Just as I believe that Taoist principles, attitudes, and practices can play a major part in our planet's future survival—if there *is* to be a future; if there *is* to be survival—so do I believe that the wisdom, spiritual beliefs, Earth-appreciation, and Earth-knowledge of the Original Americans can do the same. And I don't mean a superficial New Age, generic, white-man version of native teachings; I mean the real ones. Earth-appreciation, Earth-wisdom, and pro-Earth action can take our nation into the future. Without them, America will end up on the toxic trash-heap of misguided-human history, and our planet will end up as a dead world of dust and poisoned water, baked by the sun.

I believe that we owe both our severely wounded planet and the *most*-forgotten of forgotten Americans an immense apology and an enormous amount of help.

42.
ONE, TWO, AND THREE
LOSS AND GAIN
FORCEFUL AND UNBENDING

The Way gave birth to The One;
The One gave birth to The Two;
The Two gave birth to The Three;
The Three gave birth to the ten
Thousand things.

If you ask ten Taoists for an explanation of the above "family tree" of creation, you may hear ten different explanations—in part because Taoists are by nature individualists, in part because nobody knows for certain what the author means in this case by "The One," "The Two," and "The Three." He doesn't bother to tell us.

Since The Way of Heaven must be what the first line refers to as "The Way"—considering that The Way of Heaven started everything—then what is "The One"? Elsewhere in the chapters, *The Way of Heaven* is "The One." As for "The Two," the majority opinion of *Tao Te Ching* interpreters and commentators seems to be that they are The Dark and The Light, *yin* and *yang*. But are they necessarily what the author meant? And what are "The Three"? The usual answer is the old Chinese standby phrase, "heaven, earth, and man." But, one might well ask, what's *man* doing there? From the beginning, man has produced *his own* kind—now far more than Earth can handle—but no other kind; and he has a disturbing tendency to *injure* and *destroy* the ten thousand things. I, for one, don't think he belongs there. Maybe heaven and earth do, though. And maybe a more likely third piece of the philosophical puzzle can be found:

The Chinese love numbers—number games, explanations of this and that through numbers, and so on. For example, it's been determined that the *Way Virtue Classic* was divided into its present eighty-one chapters (in around 50 BCE) because the number nine, which represents complete, perfect *yang* in the philosophy of the *I Ching*, multiplied by itself creates a perfect number. (Also: 3 x the three-*yang*-line *I Ching* trigram for "heaven" = 9; 9 × 9 = 81.)

Chinese philosophy, loving numbers, loves groupings of three. "Heaven, earth, and man" is only one of several groupings referred to as *san yüan*, "three origins." Maybe the author of the *Tao Te Ching* had another "three origins" in mind for "The Three":

In the folk religion of China, which the author borrowed from and simplified to form some of his philosophy, there were what have become known as the *san kuan*, the "Three Rulers": *t'ien kuan*, "Heaven Ruler"; *ti kuan*, "Earth Ruler"; and *shui kuan*, "Water Ruler." In religious Taoism, which developed after philosophical Taoism, the Three Rulers were venerated as deities, with halls and temples dedicated to them. But ages before that, and during the time that the *Tao Te Ching* was apparently written, what were later called the *san kuan* were simply the powers of heaven, earth, and water.

The following is my explanatory version of the opening lines of Chapter Forty-Two:

In the pre-time of no existence, *tao*, "The Way," created itself, forming The One. The One created *yin* and *yang* and set them spinning and chasing each other, forming the *t'ai chi*, the "Supreme Ultimate"—The Two. The Two created the *san yüan*, the "three origins," known as *t'ien*, *ti*, and *shui*—heaven, earth, and water, The Three. The Three created the *wan wu*, the "ten thousand things."

In the text of my first section's second stanza, the author is, I believe, describing the practice of basic *ch'i*-directing, the foundation for Taoist martial arts and yoga: *wan* ("ten thousand") *wu* ("things") *fu* ("carry on the back") *yin* ("The Dark") *erh* ("and") *pao* ("carry in the lap") *yang* ("The Light"). This energy-circulation is said to have been developed by the ancients who observed the way that animals breathe. In practice the *ch'i* is pulled up the back on inhalation (drawing the breath in is *yin*, The Dark) to a point on the head. Then on exhalation (pushing the breath out is *yang*, The Light) the *ch'i* is dropped down to a point on the abdomen, from where it is drawn on the next inhalation. This energy circle is referred to as "the water wheel." So in basic *ch'i* circulation, practitioners "carry The Dark on their backs and carry The Light in their laps."

In the text of line four of that stanza, *ch'ung* ("water" plus "center") can be translated literally as "whirlpool" (see my notes on Chapter Four). In the stanza's context, "rotate," from *ch'ung*'s meaning of *water rotating around a center*—in this case, in "the water wheel"—seemed the most appropriate interpretation: "They rotate the two energies."

In the text of my second section's third line, the author or a copyist uses *kung*, "duke[s]," rather than the author's usual *hou*, "prince[s]."

In the fourth line, I added "when they show courtesy to others," a qualification that would have been assumed by Asian readers but not by Western readers.

In the same section's last two lines, I replaced the text's "Therefore, things perhaps diminish themselves but profit, perhaps profit themselves but diminish."

Most interpretations of the text of the first line of my third section say "What others teach I also teach," or an equivalent. Although that's an accurate translation of the text as the sentence exists today, I mentally added *chiang* (indicates future action) to the text, producing "What others teach I will teach also"—thereby bringing the sentence grammatically in line with the stanza's final sentence, wu ("I") *chiang* ("will") *i* ("use") *wei* ("to be") *chiao* ("doctrine") *fu* ("father"): "I will use that to be the father of my doctrine." One or two other interpretations I've seen make use of that consistent future-tense wording. After all, it doesn't make sense for the author to say "What others teach I also [present tense] teach," follow that declaration with what appears to be a saying of the day, and then say in conclusion that he *will* (future tense) use that saying as the father (the authoritative source) of his teaching doctrine.

Aside from the possibility that *chiang* was accidentally left out of the first sentence by a sloppy copyist is the possibility that someone, believing that the author was the alleged "Old Master," a teacher—traditionally in China, one is not designated a philosophy *master* ("Master K'ung," "Master Chuang") unless one *teaches*—eliminated *chiang* from the first sentence on the assumption that its presence was a mistake.

In historical reality, the author by all appearances taught no one, had no followers, and founded no school. Therefore, the future tense would logically be the intended one—the author is indicating that he plans to, or at least wants to, teach. But, as history seems to show, something went wrong. (Further on in the chapters and my chapter notes are indications of what that something might have been.)

Finally, "forceful and unbending" in the second line of my third section is my interpretation of *ch'iang* ("force," "to force," "forceful") *liang* ("ridgepole," "beam"). In my understanding, the latter character in that context signifies *someone who is strong but inflexible*.

For an explanation of why the author planned to use the saying "Those who are forceful and unbending do not die natural deaths" as the "father" of his doctrine, see my notes for Chapter Fifty-Five.

43.
WITHOUT EFFORT

Both water and The Way (first stanza) demonstrate the effectiveness of effortless action. Both (second stanza) teach without words. Few people learn from their teachings. But the rest of creation does.

44.
WHICH DO YOU LOVE MORE?

Ming, in the text of my first stanza's first line, can mean "name," "title," "designation," "fame," "reputation," "rank," or "position. "Position" seemed the most appropriate definition in context.

Also in line one, "self" seemed the appropriate definition of *shên*, "self" or "body." In line two, I chose "body," which I interpreted as "health."

The text of my third stanza's two final lines is *k'o i chang chiu*, "able to use *I* to adopt grow long time," which I interpreted as "[If you are] able to adopt [these principles, you will] grow [for a] long time." Other interpretations say things like "You will long endure."

From Dr. Yi Wu's notes on the chapter in his book *The Book of Lao Tzu* (Great Learning Publishing Company, San Francisco, 1989):

3. One who loves anything too much will neglect the basic principles. Material gain comes at the expense of spiritual depletion.

4. Hoarding of money and goods makes them useless. The more in storage, the greater the loss.

45.
DELETED

In Chapter Forty-One, as explained in my notes for that chapter, I eliminated a lengthy passage that seemed to be the work of someone of the School of Names. Well, in Chapter Forty-Five, whoever-it-was showed up again with another parade of paradoxes, taking up the whole of the chapter with ridiculous assertions such as "Great debating skill seems hesitant and inarticulate." (He overreached himself with that one—*nobody* will accept *that* as true.) So I threw him out again.

When the alleged Chapter Forty-Five is eliminated, there is nothing interrupting the author's "If you know what is enough" train of thought that begins in Chapter Forty-Four and concludes in Chapter Forty-Six.

46.
ENOUGH

Other people attempt to live their lives backwards; they try to have more things or more money, in order to do more of what they want, so they will be happier. The way it actually works is the reverse. You must first be who you really are, then do what you need to do, In order to have what you want.
MARGARET MEAD

The greatest discovery of any generation is that human beings can alter their lives by altering their attitudes.
ALBERT SCHWEITZER

In chapter after chapter of the *Tao Te Ching*, the author shows that man's fatal flaw is *greed*. When and where greed appears, disaster eventually follows. But greed, indicates the author here and there, can be overcome—from within, through self-discipline, meditation, and emulating The Way; and externally, through reforming rulers and governments.

47.
WITHOUT GOING

Like Chapter Ten and Chapter Sixteen, Chapter Forty-Seven seems to be concerned with meditation. But here the writing appears to be nudging people to shift their perspective and move out of socially encouraged rush-rush, look-look, go-here-go-there, strive-strive behavior. The chapter's statements go beyond everyday reality to a deeper level. They say: *Be where you are.* And: *The farther afield you go in search of the meaning of life, the less likely you'll be to find it.*

Working on this chapter, I gained the impression that, as with Chapter Nine, it might be the creation of another writer—in this case, perhaps, someone more introspective and less occupied with observing the world than is the author of the chapters I consider authentic. But, unlike the chapters I eliminated, this one contains valuable wisdom. So, as with Chapter Nine, I chose not to eliminate it but to modify its not-consistently skillful wording to make it fit better with the chapters I consider authentic.

My basic translation of the text, with English-language articles and apparently missing words (characters) added, was:

Not going out [the] door,
[One can] know under heaven.
Not watching [through the] window,

[One can] see Heaven['s] Way.
He [who] goes out [for] much distance
[Is] he [who] knows much less.

Rightly [and] accordingly [or "Thus accordingly"],
[The] wise man:
[Does] not step [out], yet knows;
[Does] not see, yet names;
[Does] not do, yet accomplishes.

Regarding "know" in the above first stanza, second line: In such a case, *chih*, "know," can be translated as either "possess knowledge of" or "possess understanding of." One cannot be familiar with or understand the world without going out in it, but one can know *about* it—possess knowledge of it—from various sources. So "know of the ways of the world" became the wording I used.

In the text of the stanza's fourth line, *chien* commonly means "to see"—but it also can mean "to perceive, be aware of." No one, according to what's said in Chapter Fourteen, can literally *see* The Way of Heaven. So I chose "perceive" as the appropriate interpretation.

I reworded the stanza's two final lines in order to avoid their awkwardness in English. And I interpreted *chih*, "knows," in that second context as "understands."

In the above second stanza's fourth line, the chapter's author—whoever he is—writes that the wise man "does not see [or "perceive"], yet names." I changed "see/perceive" to "look out" and changed "names" to "perceives," so the points made in the second stanza could be consistent with those made in the first one.

48.

DECREASE

In the pursuit of knowledge, the diligent student adds things every day.
K'UNG FU-TZŬ

Chapter Forty-Eight would appear to be a reaction to the strivings of the Confucianists, who, from the author's point of view, wanted to run the nation with "busyness"—my in-this-context interpretation of *shih*, "business," "affairs," "matters."

In my first stanza's first two lines, I interpreted *wei* ("do," "act," etc.) as "pursue" in the first line and as "follow" in the second.

The text of the stanza's last two lines is *i chih yü wu wei wu wei erh wu pu wei*, which translates as:

in order to   arrive   at   without/absence of/non-being/nothingness
    do/act/etc.
without/absence of/non-being/nothingness   do/act/etc.   but/yet/and/then
    without/absence of/non-being/nothingness   not   do/act/etc.

The traditional interpretation is along the lines of "in order to arrive at non-doing [or "not-doing"]. Then nothing is done, yet nothing is not done [or "When nothing is done, nothing is left undone"]."

The traditional rendering of *wu* as "non" or "not" in its initial appearance in the above interpretation and as "nothing" twice after that bothered me, as did the idea that when one does nothing, then nothing remains undone. Do the wise do *nothing*? Does doing nothing leave *nothing* undone? In Chapter Seventy-Seven, the author states that "[The] wise man acts, but [does] not rely on [action]." In Chapter Eighty-One, he states that "[The] wise man's way acts, but [does] not contend." So with those statements in mind, I tried a stricter interpretation of the characters: "in order to arrive at without-doing—without doing, yet without not-doing." Which—as with the similar wording in Chapter Thirty-Seven—evolved into: "in order to arrive at *without-striving*—without *striving*, yet without *not-acting*."

Wu wei erh wu pu wei—*without doing, yet without not-doing:* The phrase is about *efficiency*—the fluid, effortless, egoless efficiency of nature, not the busy-busy, stuffed-minded, stiff "efficiency" of Confucianism at one extreme or do-nothing laziness at the other. To attain that efficiency of nature, "Decrease, then again decrease, in order to arrive at *without-striving*."

I interpreted *t'ien hsia*, "under heaven," in the text of my second stanza's first line as "the nation"—the sociopolitical realm—rather than as "the world" as other interpretations present it, because the chapter seems directed at the Confucianists, who wanted to take over the nation, not the world. The author giving advice on how to take over the world seems, to say the least, out of character.

The second stanza's text, in my translation, reads: "To take hold of under heaven, always use without-business. Reaching for it having business [will] not [be] sufficient in order to take hold of under heaven."

Incidentally: According to *The American Heritage Dictionary of the English Language,* the original meaning of "business" was "The condition of being busy. [Middle English *businesse*, from *bisi*, busy.]"

For more on effortless action—"doing without doing"—see Chapter Sixty-Three and its notes.

49.
VIRTUE
THE WISE MAN

As Chapter Forty-Nine contains two themes—one of autobiographical statements concerning Virtue and one describing the behavior of a wise man—I decided to separate the two. The Chinese text consists of the characters of my second section's first two lines, followed by those of my entire first section, which are followed by those of the remaining lines of my second section—mixing the "I" theme with the "wise man" theme. The result is scatterbrained and conceited writing alien to the author's obviously non-scatterbrained writing style and obviously non-conceited character—which to me means that someone early on scrambled together two sets of statements, an "I" set and a "he" set.

Regarding the now-first section: The author is saying that Virtue is not a "now it's on, now it's off" sort of thing—inconsistent goodness is not goodness, inconsistent sincerity is not sincerity. With Virtue, including goodness and sincerity, it needs to be there all the time or it's nothing. Anything less than full-time is a fraud. By that standard, the Confucianists, with their measured-out and conditional behavior and treatment of individuals, were perpetrating a great deception.

As for the now-second section: In the text of my third line, the phrase *shêng jên*, "wise man," is followed by *tsai*, the original, pictographic meaning of which was "to exert one's intelligence, talents, or presence on a place."

The characters of the third-from-last line of my second section are not present in the standard Wang Pi text (all are present in two other old texts; some are present in one other), but Wang Pi commented on them as if they were before him as he wrote—which would seem to indicate that his copy of the text was later copied and passed down without them.

A final thought: It would seem unlikely that any citizen of the world could read Chapter Forty-Nine and not think of Mahatma Gandhi and His Holiness the Dalai Lama.

50.
ONE IN TEN

In my first stanza, third and fourth lines, "foot soldiers" is my in-this-chapter's-context interpretation of *t'u*, "to go on foot," "foot soldier," "disciple," "apprentice." One analytical dictionary stated that the character's literal meaning is "to go on the ground"—in this case signifying, I believe, *those of lesser importance than those who ride*.

In the sixth and ninth lines of my first stanza and the last line of my second stanza, "death place" (*ssu ti*) is, it seems to me, something internal created by desires and fears.

My possibly unique interpretation of the text of my first stanza's lines ten and eleven, "It is because they live lives that grow too rich and sheltered," is based on the text's *i* ("because" *ch'i* ("they") *shêng* ("live") *shêng* ("lives") *chih* (the original meanings of which were "to grow, to develop," "to continue, to progress") *hou* ("thick," "generous," "large," "very," "rich") *kai* ("to cover," "a covering," "a roof").

As I interpret what the author is saying, the "foot soldiers of life" desire security and fear risk, including that of death. They are not self-directed, but are commanded by those more powerful than themselves. The "foot soldiers of death" fear the pressures of life and desire self-obliteration, such as through alcohol or other drugs, perpetual busyness, or dangerous activities. They too are not self-directed. They avoid silence and solitude, because these force them to face the emptiness of their inner lives. "Those who move to a death place" desire material riches, power, acclaim, and prestige, and fear the loss of them. Although they may ride through life in roofed carriages, they end up no better off internally than the "foot soldiers of death," because the material riches, power, acclaim, and prestige they acquire don't bring them what they need, but only bring them what they want.

The question in the text of my first stanza's lines seven through nine (*fu ho ku*, "[As for] the ones in question, what reason?") seems to refer to "those [in the previous sentence] who move to a death place," as the answer that follows apparently does not apply to the "foot soldiers." So I interpreted the question as "As for these last three in ten, for what reason do they move to a death place?" Also, I added a final line to the stanza, to lead into the second stanza. Except for those two wording changes, my interpretation is, I believe, as close to an accurate character-by-character translation as is possible–for example, my possibly unique "From coming forth at birth to entering the ground at death": *ch'u* ("come forth") *shêng* ("produce," "life," "birth") *ju* ("enter"–pictorially, *roots entering ground*) *ssu* (death").

To help clarify what the author is saying in the text of my second stanza:

The author John Blofeld, who spent time in various Taoist (*tao-chiao*) monasteries in China before the Communist takeover of the nation and assault on Taoism, wrote of a literally face-to-face encounter with a tiger while traveling in a remote area of China. Realizing that there was no chance of escape, feeling no fear but only admiration for the magnificent being confronting him, he knelt and touched his forehead to the ground in respect. The tiger licked his face and moved on.

51.
THE TEN THOUSAND THINGS

The standard Wang Pi text of my second stanza contains two characters not found in some other texts' versions of the chapter.

The first of these is *t'ing*, among the various definitions of which are "straight" and "firm." I interpreted *t'ing* in context as "strengthen" (line three). Instead of *t'ing*, some other *Tao Te Ching* texts have *ch'êng*, "to complete," "to finish," "to become." But *ch'êng* is already used in the text of my first stanza, line four (I interpret it as "develop"), in which it is attributed to *circumstances*—so it can't very well be attributed in this second stanza to Virtue without creating a conflict.

The second of the two characters is *tu*, "poison," which makes an English-language version of the text of part of the second stanza read: "Virtue feeds them, grows them . . . poisons them. . . ." As Wang Pi was not known to have had a warped sense of humor, the natural assumption is that someone made a mistake. And to my way of thinking the most likely possibility is that someone mistakenly wrote *tu,* "poison," rather than *tu*, "oversee, superintend, watch over." I substituted the latter character, choosing the definition "watch over" (second stanza, line four).

Instead of *tu*, "poison," some other texts have *shou*, "ripen." But, although "ripen" is an appropriate choice for fruit-growing—as well as a positive alternative to Virtue poisoning the ten thousand things—it seems an odd choice in the context of a sentence of terms applicable to *all* of the various forms of life.

52.
THE WORLD'S MOTHER

From the various commentaries I've read on Chapter Fifty-Two, as well as the various interpretations I've read of it, I would say that among scholars and translators it's considered the greatest enigma in the *Way Virtue Classic*. Like Chapter One, it could be called a riddle in essay form. Yet, like Chapter One—as I believe my true-to-the-characters translation/interpretation of this chapter shows—it's very simple.

As have the creators of most English-language interpretations I've seen, I interpreted *t'ien hsia* ("under heaven") in the text of my first stanza's lines one and two as meaning "the world." But, unlike most of them, I interpreted *tzŭ*, "child" or "children," in the text of lines four and five as meaning "child" rather than "children"—the world (*t'ien hsia*), not the ten thousand things (*wan wu*).

As I interpret the text of my first stanza, the author is saying that when we know The Mother (*t'ien hsia mu*, "heaven-under mother"), we will know her child, the world. (Because in the case of *this* mother and *this* child, The Mother—the spirit, The Way—is within the child.) When we know the child, and thereby realize how special it is, we will protect the spirit within it and beyond it. (For an explanation of *shou*, "guard," "protect," or "keep," as "protect"—typically interpreted in this case and some others as "keep" or "keep to"—see my notes for Chapter Thirty-Two.) I added "you," "you will," and "your" to the stanza to make it work better in English.

In the second-to-last line of my first stanza, "You will repeatedly protect The Mother," "repeatedly" is my in-context interpretation of *fu*, "to return," "to repeat." Other interpreters have either interpreted *fu* as "return"—"return and keep to the mother"—or have seemingly ignored its presence.

In my second stanza, the author recommends going within ("Stop your pleasant words, shut your gate") and getting acquainted with The Mother, rather than lose touch with her by "start[ing] your pleasant words and further[ing] your affairs" like a talky-talky, busy-busy Confucianist.

The phrase "pleasant words" in lines one and three is from *yüeh*, the ancient ancestor of the "borrowed" character *tui* (the same character, but newer definitions). *Yüeh* meant "nice words," "good words that dispel grief and rejoice the hearer." Apparently because its brush-written descendant's meanings—"exchange," "barter," "pay," "deliver"—make no sense in this context, and because the character contains the representation of a mouth, *yüeh/tui* tends to be (out of desperation, I suppose) interpreted in this chapter and elsewhere as "mouth," "openings," or "passages."

In line three, "start" is from *k'ai*, "to open," "to begin," typically interpreted as "open" (goes with "mouth," "openings," or "passages").

In my third stanza, "perceiving" in line one is from *chien*, "to see," "to perceive," "to apprehend," "to be aware of."

In line two, "protecting" is from *shou*, "to guard," "to protect," "to keep," as in the first stanza. The typical interpretation, as noted for the first stanza, is "keeping," "keeping to," or the like.

In line three, I interpreted *ch'i*—"it," "he," "she," and by extension "its," "his," "her"—as "her," which I then interpreted as "The Great Mother" (The Way), because that seemed to be what was referred to in lines one and two as *hsiao*, "[the] small" (see Chapter Thirty-Two, Chapter Thirty-Four) and *jou*, "[the] soft" (see Chapter Six). In the next line, I interpreted *ch'i* as "her" for the same reason as above.

In line four, "repeatedly returning" is my interpretation of *fu* ("return" or "repeat") *kuei* ("return"). Other editions present an interpretation of only one of the two characters, presumably due to having translated both as "return" and ending up with "return return" or "returning returning."

"Without leaving your troubles behind" (line five) is my possibly unique interpretation of *wu i shên yang*, "without lose/forget/leave behind self/body misfortune."

In the final line, "is said to be merely *practicing* constancy" is my possibly unique interpretation of *shih wei hsi ch'ang*, "Is said to practice constancy." *Hsi*, "to practice," depicts young birds learning to fly. I added "merely" and emphasized "practicing" to make clearer what I believe the author is saying—that to neglect to leave personal problems behind when engaging in meditation is not *performing* constancy (union with The Changeless Way) but is only *practicing* (meaning *rehearsing* or *learning*) it.

The typical interpretation of the text of my third stanza's last four lines goes like this: "Using brightness [eliminates *ch'i*, "her"], return [eliminates *fu,* "repeat"] to enlightenment [eliminates a second *ch'i*]. Do not [changes *wu*, "without," to "do not"] bring trouble upon yourself [changes *i shên yang*, "leaving behind self-misfortune" to "bring trouble upon yourself"]. This is called 'practicing [meaning *performing*] constancy.'"

In his notes on the chapter, James Legge writes: "The meaning of the chapter is obscure, and the commentators give little help in determining it." Simply put, those who do not grasp what the author says elsewhere about The Way's presence in everything, and about the importance of protecting it, will not understand this chapter.

Many who have had near-death experiences have reported that after leaving their bodies they had entered a realm in which they felt surrounded by *unconditional love*, like that of a mother for her children—with no strings attached, no fatherly-disciplinary "I will love you *if* you do this, or *if* you don't do that." Such, it would seem, is the character of The Way of Heaven. With all due respect to the father-figure religion I grew up in, I would say that if the universe were ruled by anything but a mother-natured spirit, the Earth-destructive, ten-thousand-things-destructive, people-destructive human race would have been eliminated from this world long ago.

In her book *Angels in My Hair* (Harmony Books, New York, 2008, 2011), Irish Catholic seer Lorna Byrne tells of the following childhood experience:

> Sometimes when I was alone on the swing one of the angels would say, "Lorna, stretch out your hand. We have something to show you." Then the angel would put something tiny in my hand, and a light would start to materialize there. . . . [T]his light would start to grow, almost as if it were coming alive. As it grew and grew it started to glow and a bright yellow light came from it. The light rose up from my hand and went upward, getting bigger and brighter all the time until it partially obscured the sun. Then I would see a most wonderful sight reflected back, as if through a mirror—a beautiful face, like a human face, smiling down at me.
>
> The first time this happened the angels . . . explained that this person was the Queen of the Angels, the mother of the universe, the mother of creation, the mother of all the angels. All of a sudden the yellow orb in which I had seen the face exploded into millions of little pieces and fell like golden streamers coming from the sun.

Over the years the angels have regularly given me this gift, even as an adult, particularly when I've been in need of some reassurance.

53.
THE SHORTEST PATH

In my first stanza, "Supposing that I had a little glimmer of awareness" is from the text's *shih wo chieh jan yu chih*, "Supposing that I [a] little light have/had [of] knowing." "Travel only on The Great Way" is from *hsing yü ta tao wei*, "walk on Great Way only." (In Chinese character-order, generally speaking, *wei*, "only," follows rather than precedes what it modifies.) "Giving it the greatest respect" is from *shih shih wei* (a different *wei* character), "giving absolute dread/respect/awe." The typical interpretation of the text goes something like: "If I had even a little bit of wisdom, I would walk on the Great Way, and only fear to stray from it."

The text of the last three lines of the stanza is *ta tao shên erh min hao ching*, which I translated as "Great Way very easy, but the people / the multitude fond of shortest way." That made no sense to me when I considered the rest of the chapter's statements, as it's the elegantly dressed, wealthy few—not the people, the multitude—who are being described as robbers. (Some interpreters get around that problem by presenting *min* as simply "people." But that doesn't work, either—the described robbers aren't just "people.")

When I researched the character *min*, I found in an analytical dictionary the claim that *min* can be "analogous to *shih*, 'clan, family'"—which I suppose means that *min* in this case could be a way of saying "my people," "the family," or "the clan." The two characters, I saw, belong to the same "radical" (root-meaning) group. And I noticed that:

Min's ancient ancestor differs from *shih*'s by its top line doubling back below itself, and by its lower-placed horizontal line. I wondered if an early copyist could have misread *shih*—or, believing that the author was in truth someone styled "Old Master," had decided that *shih*, "clan, family," must have been a mistake and had consequently written *min*, instead. In any event, "the clan, the family" worked in the chapter's context and "the people, the multitude" did not. And that brings the author's critical description of the men in my third stanza very close to home, as does another chapter further on.

The text of the melancholy, interlude-like second stanza's first line is *ch'ao shên ch'ü*, "Royal court very removed / taken away / subtracted," which I interpreted as "The royal court is very neglected." (I ended up leaving the repetitive "very" out of each of the stanza's lines.) The last character, *ch'ü*, Is the opposite of *yü*, "surplus, excess." *Ch'ao*, now meaning "imperial court," was the court of "the Son of Heaven," the Chou Dynasty's king, at Loyang. (In the dynasty that would follow—the unifying Ch'in Dynasty, from which would come our name *China*—the title "the Son of Heaven" would be taken by the first emperor, Ch'in Shih-huang-ti, and would be the title of all emperors after him.)

"Rob-and-boasters" in my third stanza's seventh line is my interpretation of *tao* ("rob, robber") *k'ua* ("to speak loudly," "to boast," "conceited").

In the chapter's ending, the author plays on the same-sounding but very differently written *tao*, "robbers," and *tao*, "The Way," saying—with emphasis—that the *tao k'ua*, the "rob-and-boasters," are *not tao*, not followers of The Way. The two final lines are my version of that ending.

The "picture" that the author presents in this chapter and elsewhere is that of factionalist greed and contention, neglect of and overtaxation of the majority, and the absence of a powerful, unifying central government, national law and order, and social stability. Such was the nation-of-states that the author lived in—not greatly unlike ours today (2020).

54.
CULTIVATE GROWTH

In his notes on this chapter, James Legge expresses doubt, using the word *peculiar*, about a sentence following the text of my first stanza. That part of the text seemed to me to have been added by someone—a Confucianist, I would say, from the wording. A few interpreters have chosen to de-Confucianize the questioned sentence (Gia-fu Feng's version is one I especially like). However, the statement as written didn't fit with what preceded and followed it; and, I decided, no matter how I reworded it, it wouldn't be necessary. So I eliminated it.

"Growth" in my second stanza is my in-that-context interpretation of *chih*, which originally meant "growth," "development," "progress," and which then came to mean "he," "she," "it," or the possessive sign, as well. Brush-written Chinese uses the last four definitions only. Other interpretations of the text of my second stanza present *chih* as either "it" or "Virtue," either of which necessitates the rewriting of each of the text's statements.

As I understand the statements in the text of my third stanza—a basic translation of which would be "According to self, consider self. According to family, consider family," and so on—the author is saying that the individual needs to be considered according to what's healthy and appropriate for the individual (not for the family, the community, etc.); that the family needs to be considered according to what's healthy and appropriate for the family (not for the community, the nation, etc.); and so on. Confucianism, by contrast, saw the individual as someone to fit into the family, the family as something to fit into the community, and the community as something to fit into the nation. And there the Confucianists stopped, with the nation. But, indicates the author here and elsewhere, there is also *the world*—what is healthy and appropriate for *the world*?

In the text following that of my third stanza was a ten-character restatement of the eleven-character ending of Chapter Twenty-One. It didn't seem to fit with the rest of this chapter, so I eliminated it.

55.

LIKE A BABY

In my first stanza, "abundance" in line one is my in-that-context interpretation of *hou*, "thick," "large," "generous," "very," "rich."

I added lines three and four because without them the description that follows the chapter's opening statement misleadingly appears at first to be that of an adult, rather than a baby. (Was something left out of the text?)

In the text of lines eleven and twelve, "He does not yet know the union of male and female," "male" is *mu*, "the male of quadrupeds," "a bull," "generic male"; "female" is *p'in*, "the female of animals," "a cow," "generic female"—not *nan* ("man") and *nü* ("woman") as several other interpretations imply.

The following line, "And so acts in wholeness," is my interpretation of *erh ch'uan tso*, the definitions of which are:

thus   all/the whole/complete   to act/to do/to make/arise/appear/arouse

Most old texts of the chapter (most of the few *surviving* ones) have instead of *ch'üan*, "wholeness," as in the standard Wang Pi text and some others, the character *tsui*, "male organ." I consider *tsui* to be either a mistake or a misguided change, one that leads rather grotesquely away from what the author appears to me to be saying. Several English-language interpreters have adopted *tsui*—possibly because they follow majority rule or scholarly precedent (both of which, as I've shown elsewhere, can be wrong and often are), or possibly because the standard text's *ch'üan*, "wholeness," didn't make sense to them. It makes perfect sense to me (I'll show why a bit further on); but then, I'm a Taoist, which puts me in a very small minority (three?) among English-language interpreters of the *Way Virtue Classic*. (It would seem that the number-one qualification for translators/interpreters of the *Tao Te Ching* is *that they not be Taoists*. Confucianists, yes; Buddhists, yes; Christians, yes; non-Taoist academics, yes; non-Taoist Chinese, yes; Taoists, no.)

Interpretation matters like the one just mentioned could be said to demonstrate what happens when one interprets, or changes, the characters of a passage by focusing solely on the characters. One must also take into consideration what the characters mean in the context of the chapter and in the context of the author's statements throughout the work. At the same time, one must be careful to exclude attitudes expressed in the works of later Taoist writers—a discipline not practiced, according to what I've seen, by other *Tao Te Ching* interpreters, who tend to interpret the *Way Virtue Classic* according to the writings of Chuang-tzŭ (Chuang Chou), whose reject-all-involvement, *literally* do-nothing Taoism radically differs from the reform-the-rulers, fix-the-problems, work-with-nature Taoism expressed by the author of the *Tao Te Ching*.

Ch'üan, "wholeness," seems to me to be the chapter's key concept. Wholeness was an important concept to emphasize to the male readers of the *Tao Te Ching* (it would not be until the Sung Dynasty (960–1279 CE) that any more than a small minority of women would be taught to read and write) because to the author, as he makes clear in various chapters, it's not enough to just "be a man"—to follow the attitude dominant then, and still dominant now, that limits the human male animal to the ideal or stereotype of being physically strong (but rigid), mentally inflexible, and emotionally constricted. As the text of my third stanza points out, having only that robust male strength (*chuang*, "strong," "robust," "vigorous," "stout," "thick plank," in the text of my first two lines) wears one out too soon. Women outlive men, as water outlasts stone. So a wise man works with that *yin* lesson of nature to become flexible and yielding. One then develops a more balanced, longer-lived strength—not merely *muscle* strength, but life-sustaining *ch'i* strength. *Yang* plus *yin* equals *wholeness*.

As this chapter points out, *ch'i* strength, life-energy strength, is like that of a baby. Anyone who has ever tried to open a baby's clenched fist has learned how strong a baby can be. A healthy baby has very small muscles but very powerful *ch'i*. *Ch'i Kung* (Taoist yoga) and the Taoist martial arts have that soft but firm *ch'i* strength as their goal.

"Developing" (fourth line from the end of my first stanza) and "growing toward" (the final line) are from the original meanings of *chih*—"grow, develop," "continue, progress." Other translations neglect the character.

Lines three through four of my second stanza differ from all other interpretations I've seen. I simply followed the characters. Other English-language versions interpret the last character in the text of my line three, *hsiang* ("felicity," "good fortune") as "ominous," "bad omen," and the like. (*Hsiang* is composed of *shih*, "a revelation," plus *yang*, "sheep," and means "a fortunate or auspicious revelation.") They also treat as negative the statement that in line four I give as "To-send-energy-with-the-mind is called *power*." (The characters of that statement are *hsin shih ch'i yüeh ch'iang*, "mind caused/sent energy called powerful.") The first of the two negative interpretations is by the long-standing definitions of the characters insupportable; the second shows a non-Taoist ignorance of the importance of *ch'i*-circulation exercises—which Chapter Ten and Chapter Forty-Two indicate the author himself practiced—in attaining *wholeness*.

A possible reason for the negative interpretations of those statements is that early English-language interpreters may have read them as criticisms of the elaborate *tao-chiao* (Taoist religion) meditation / inner alchemy practices, thereby setting a trend for the interpreters who came after them to follow. *Tao-chiao* practitioners have traditionally believed, or have wanted to believe, that they could attain physical immortality—not merely longevity—through this or that application of *ch'i* exercises, a goal that *tao-chia* (Taoist philosophy) practitioners have traditionally considered futile and a waste of time and *ch'i*. But there are two difficulties with that possible explanation: first, the characters say what they say, not the opposite; second, when the work later titled the *Tao Te Ching* was written, neither *tao-chia* nor *tao-chiao* had come into existence.

Another (probably more likely) reason is that, as I said earlier, other interpreters tend to interpret the *Tao Te Ching* according to the philosophy of Chuang-tzŭ. Master Chuang made fun of physical and "breathing" (*ch'i*-circulating) exercises and those who practiced them. But Master Chuang did not write the *Tao Te Ching*.

56.

DEEP UNITY

In the text of my second stanza, the author takes some of what he said in Chapter Fifty-Two a bit further, saying: *Stop all chatter, shut yourself away, and go within until you reach Deep Unity (hsüan t'ung). This unity-with-everything will give you no usual-values advantages, but it will give you something better.*

As in Chapter Fifty-Two, "pleasant words" in the first line of that stanza is the meaning of *yüeh*, the ancient ancestor of the text's *tui*.

The line following my second stanza is my alternative to the text's *ku*, "consequently" or "as a result of that."

My translation of the text of my next stanza, which at first left the character *erh* untranslated, was:

not able [to] get *erh* closeness
not able [to] get *erh* distance
not able [to] get *erh* profit
not able [to] get *erh* injury
not able [to] get *erh* honor
not able [to] get *erh* disgrace

Of the definitions of *erh* ("and," "but," "yet," "then," "thus," "In those circumstances," "still," "also"), both "then" and "in those circumstances" seemed reasonable choices, producing: "Not able to get then/in those circumstances closeness [etc.]"—or, in standard

English, "not able to then/in those circumstances get closeness [etc.]." After trying several wording choices, I settled on: "You will not be able to gain closeness from it; you will not be able to gain distance" and so on.

That left the text of the chapter's final sentence, *ku wei t'ien hsia kuei,* "Consequently be heaven under honored/valued." The *ku* ("consequently," "as a result of that") seemed inappropriate. I wondered if there had originally been an *erh,* "but," before it—or if the *ku* had originally been *erh.* I replaced *ku*'s "as a result of that" with "but," after which the statement became understandable to me.

Although the translation and interpretation of this chapter seemed relatively straightforward, I've noticed that no two translators/interpreters seem to agree on its meanings.

57.
CAUSE AND EFFECT

The text of my first stanza's first nine lines consists only of three unattributed sayings. For clarity, I added "Confucianists have a saying," "Militarists have a saying," and "I have a saying," as well as the emphasis.

As I did in some other chapters (Chapter Forty-Eight, for example), and as explained in my notes for those chapters, I interpreted *wu* ("without," "absence of") *shih* ("business," "affairs," "matters") in the eighth line of my first stanza as "without-busyness." In the fifth line of my final stanza, I interpreted the phrase as "without busybodying."

The last line of my first stanza, "By stopping, turning, and looking," is my in-context interpretation of *i* ("by means of") *tz'ŭ,* the ancient ancestor of which, as explained in my notes for Chapter Twenty-One, meant "to stop the feet and turn."

The text of lines five through seven of my second stanza followed the text of what is now the last line of the stanza. I moved those lines to where they seemed to better fit.

In the second stanza's eighth line, "sharp operators" is my in-that-context interpretation of *li* ("sharp," "clever," "profit," "gain") *ch'i* ("utensils," "instruments," "tools," "vessels"). Most interpretations I've seen render *li ch'i* in this chapter and Chapter Thirty-Six as "sharp weapons." As explained in other chapter notes, *ch'i,* "utensils," was in ancient times a slang term for, among other people, specialists or operators. I added "manipulating the people" (next line) to help clarify my interpretation.

The text of the two lines following my second stanza is *ku* ("consequently," "therefore") *shêng* ("wise" or "holy") *jên* ("man") *yu* ("say," "says," "said"). It seemed obvious from what follows those characters that this "wise man" is a wise *ruler.* (Was the text's *shêng jên,* I wondered, originally *shêng wang,* "sage-king"?) So I changed the wording accordingly and added "rule" after "I" in the first of the quoted lines that follow, to fill in what seemed to be a missing character. I added "act" in the fifth line and "live" in the seventh line for the same reason.

Most interpretations of the above "wise man/ruler" statement say "Therefore the sage says," or "Therefore the Sage says." But who is "the sage," or "the Sage"? At least some interpreters seem to believe that the author is referring *to himself*—uncharacteristically immodest behavior for any Chinese, and certainly uncharacteristic of the author. Why would he, having used *wu*, "I," in the text of my first stanza, now refer to himself as "the sage"? If the text's *shêng jên* is an unspecified wise man, wouldn't "a sage" be the appropriate wording?

James Legge presents the phrase in question as "Therefore a sage has said," and in his notes on the chapter states: "We do not know if the author were quoting any particular sage . . . or referring generally to the sages of the past." It may be that the author is doing what some other Chinese philosophers seem to have done on occasion: attribute sayings to specified or unspecified "sage-kings" or other wise men of dim and distant antiquity, thereby "validating" statements that in reality they had made up themselves.

58.

DELETED

Chapter Fifty-Eight could be summed up as *strange characters strangely applied.* In my translation, it begins:

> Its government melancholy, melancholy [or "depressed, depressed"
> or "stupid, stupid"];
> Its people simple, simple [or "honest, honest" or "pure, pure"].
> Its government examines, examines [or "considers, considers" or
> "discerns, discerns"];
> Its people lacking, lacking [or "defective, defective" or "broken,
> broken"].

And it becomes weirder as it goes along. Was its author not used to writing in Chinese? Was he ignorant of certain character-meanings?

With each examination of the chapter I became more suspicious of it, because of its vocabulary, its attitude, and its way of expressing things.

Much of its vocabulary is conspicuously—even at a glance—unlike that found in the chapters I consider authentic. Eight of its characters are found in no other chapter. Each of another eight characters is used in only one other chapter. One of the latter group of eight is used in a chapter I eliminated as inauthentic. A second is used in a chapter's section I eliminated as inauthentic. A third is present in another chapter because, I believe—as I explain in that chapter's notes—someone made a mistake while copying a similar character.

As for attitude, the chapter is bitter and cynical, creating an atmosphere of darkness and defeat. Although such an attitude might have been appropriate for someone trying to survive in the Warring States period, or for the legend's bitter, disillusioned "Old Master," it is not the attitude of the author of the *Way Virtue Classic*. *That* writer identifies problems and presents solutions—he even implies solutions by the wording of his criticisms—and describes the wise and their wisdom in ways that can be easily understood and emulated, while this chapter's author only moans about conditions and then gives a very odd, and therefore hard to learn from, description of how the wise behave:

> Therefore, wise man square but not cutting, angular but not hurting, straight but not expansive, bright but not illuminating [or "glorious"].

As regards literary expression, this chapter's wording is awkward and obscure, particularly in its puzzling use of *ch'i* ("its," "his," "her") and its questionable and confusing assertions. The result has been widely varying translations/interpretations—or, more accurately, *rewritings*—of the chapter's statements. The various commentaries on and explanations of this chapter that I've read are clever and convincing, but they have nothing to do with the actual character-meanings. If someone were to make a literal translation/interpretation of the characters, using their most likely meanings, the result would be so confusing that I doubt that anyone would be able to make sense of it. At least, *I* couldn't.

59.

RESTRAINT

The theme of this chapter seems to be that spiritual and material self-discipline greatly increase one's ability to wisely rule.

In my first stanza, I replaced "frugality" (*shê*) with "wise economy" (line three), in order to better express what I believe the author is saying.

In my second stanza, for the same reason, I replaced "frugality" with "thrift-like restraint" (line one) and added "To the childlike, uncluttered state" (line three) for clarity.

Also in the second stanza, I followed the lead of James Legge and most other interpreters of the chapter in substituting *fu*, "return," for *fu*, "to subject," "yield to." The latter character was obviously a copyist's mistake.

The character *mo*, which appears in the text of my first and third stanzas, can be read as meaning "no," "not," "none," or "nothing," or as a negative interrogative ("is it not?" and so on). To me, by context, the author clearly intends the interrogative meaning. Other interpreters of this chapter have chosen "nothing" in the first case and "none" or "no one" in the second.

So my beginning translation of the chapter's first sentence, *chih jên shih t'ien mo jo shê*, was: "Governing people, serving heaven [–] are those not like frugality?" Interpretations in other editions tend toward something like: "In governing people and in serving heaven, there is nothing like frugality." (Which gives a very different meaning to the statement, namely that one needs to be frugal in governing people and in serving heaven.) My translation of the text of line four of my third stanza, *mo chih ch'i chi*, was: "[Will] not [one] know [that] that [is the] utmost?" Interpretations in other editions run along the lines of: "No one can know where it will end." My translation of the text of the last four lines of my third stanza, *mo chih ch'i chi k'o i yu kuo*, was: "Is it not [by] knowing [that] that [is the] utmost [that one] can accordingly have [the] nation?" Interpretations in other editions vary considerably, but tend toward something like: "When one does not know limits [or "When one does not know where the limits are"], one can be the ruler of the nation." (But who would want a ruler who doesn't know limits, or know where they are?)

In my third stanza, last line, "governing" is my substitute for "having" (*yu*), as it is more active and less vague than "having."

In my fourth stanza, first line, I again replaced "having"–this time with "ruling with," which seemed more explanatory. In the same line, "The Nation's Mother" is apparently an author-devised title for The Way.

I believe that "having [or "ruling with"] The Nation's Mother" means *emulating The Way by doing what needs to be done, and no more.*

60.
THE UNHAPPY DEAD

In my first stanza of the chapter, the author remarks by analogy that the governing of a large nation is a delicate matter requiring a light, careful touch rather than extreme, heavy-handed actions. He goes on to say in the rest of the chapter that governing in accordance with The Way (with a light touch) would not only be good for the living, it would also be good for the *kuei*, the "unhappy spirits," "souls of the dead."

The *kuei*, commonly referred to as "hungry ghosts," are the spirits of people who died either tragically, violently, far from home, or without respect or after-death offerings from their descendants. The ancient form of the character *kuei* depicts a human being vanishing into the air. *Kuei* have been known to cause quite a bit of trouble for the living. Hungry ghosts, stuck between the physical world and the spirit realm, can be hungry for *energy*–so they hang about the living, leeching their energy and making them physically and emotionally enervated. Or they can be hungry for *mischief* or *revenge*, haunting places they had strong connections to and bothering those who now live there. In any case, they disrupt people's lives. The Taoist attitude is that unhappy spirits need help, not hostility—they need to be restored to harmony with The Way. A Taoist would say that the *kuei* (hungry ghosts) need *kuei* (to be restored).

In my third stanza, line two, I added "living or dead" to clarify what I believe the author means. I also added line three, "So then, under The Way," for the same reason.

In the next two lines I interpreted the text's statement, which I translated as "They both not each other injure," as "Neither the wise nor the ghosts would hurt each other."

The last three lines of the third stanza, "Virtue would bring them together / And restore harmony to the / Unhappy dead," are my interpretation of the text's cryptic *te chiao kuei*, "virtue join restore."

61.

ONE THAT LIES BELOW

The following are Dr. Yi Wu's notes on Chapter Sixty-One, from his book *The Book of Lao Tzu*:

1. *Liu* [the character of my first stanza's second line, "to flow," "to circulate," "to move about"] means to flow to a low place, the ocean or the lower parts of a river; a big state should be such a low place.

2. The low place, like an ocean, is the focal point to which all rivers flow. [The character used is *chiao*, "to cross," "crossing," the ancient ancestor of which depicts a man with crossed legs.] The relationship between the low place and the female is that both share the characteristic of tranquility. Note that, throughout Taoism, the low place . . . is characterized as both female and valuable, contrary to the general concept of lowness as inferior and therefore pejorative to the female.

3. By occupying the low place, the large state shows that it is supportive rather than aggressive; therefore, the small state is willing to be absorbed, to become a vassal of the big state.

4. As a vassal, the small state has the big state's protection.

5. [The] last line [the chapter's concluding sentence] deals only with the big state because it, having occupied a high position and having become aware of its perils, can decide which is the better of the two positions to assume.

As I understand what this chapter seems to be saying, the author means that if a state were to make itself attractive with *yin* peacefulness and humility, a neighboring state would want to join with it, as a man would want to join with an attractive, serene, very feminine woman.

As a political concept, that *yin* principle seemed a bit hard for me to grasp—accustomed as I am to living in a *yang*, military-dominated society—until I considered the Warring States period's overused and impractical alternative: for a state to expend enormous quantities of funds, energy, and lives to grab a neighboring state, and in the destructive process ruin that neighboring state and earn the hatred of its subjects—and after conquering it find itself with a tremendous burden, having to with war-reduced resources rebuild and militarily control and guard both itself and the conquered state. And because of all that find that its expanded, weakened self was vulnerable to conquest by other states. That's what the Warring States period was about—short-sighted, aggressive greed bringing about long-term danger and disaster. Compared to that behavior, this chapter's stated approach makes a good deal of sense.

Also: One might consider the long-standing alliance-by-marriage practice of the monarchies and clans of Europe and Asia, in which a small kingdom or family gains an alliance with a larger one by sending a daughter as a bride for the other's head man, or his son; and in which a large kingdom or family gains an alliance with a smaller one by the same means. In each case, the one honors the other and thereby places itself below it. And in each case, the one's daughter, through her well-bred charm and diplomacy, "uses peace and stillness to overcome the [other's possibly trouble-making] male—using her serenity, she places herself below him."

The Chinese text of my fourth stanza has been interpreted in a variety of ways. Each way I checked translates twice-given character *huo* as "state." But *huo*, I discovered, means "defended territory." With boundary lines drawn around it, *huo* becomes *kuo*, "state" or "nation" depending on context. *Huo* pictographically means *land with a castle or city wall, defended with weapons—a territory with uncertain boundaries*. My initial translation of the stanza's characters, *ku huo hsia i ch'ü huo hsia erh ch'ü*, was: "So territory lowers in order to obtain. Territory lower thus obtains."

I wondered why the author would repeat the principle already covered with *kuo*, "state," using *huo*, "territory." After all, the principle would be the same in either case. Then I noticed that *huo*, "land with uncertain boundaries," also means "by extension, an indeterminate person whose name is not given"—or, as one analytical dictionary more simply put it, "someone." Concluding that "someone" was the author's intended meaning, I modified my translation accordingly. The author, I believe, is describing the principle of personal *yin* power—useful in everything from diplomacy (gain through humility and composure) to the martial arts (gain through a lower center of gravity, enticement, and calm observation).

I added all of the chapter's emphasis.

62.
MYSTERIOUS SANCTUARY

In line one of my first stanza, "mysterious sanctuary" is my version of the text's *ao*, "dark corner"–further defined in analytical dictionaries as "quiet," "mysterious"–the part of a house in which treasured objects were traditionally stored for protection.

In line five, "sweet" is one of the original meanings of *mei*, now meaning "beautiful," "excellent." "Buy and sell" is my interpretation of *shih*, "market."

Regarding "respectful" in line six: *Tsun* is now defined as "respectable," "honorable," or "noble." But *tsun's* ancient ancestor–later changed by the scribes–depicted two hands reverently raising a ceremonial wine cup to the spirits of the dead. So I interpreted that character in its ancient form as "respectful" rather than "respectable"–which fit with what seemed yet another jab at Confucianist speech and behavior.

Also in line six, "add to them" is my interpretation of *chia*, "add," "increase," "confer upon," or "inflict," which consists of "mouth" plus "muscle." According to analytical dictionaries, the character is a picture of *adding force to words*.

In the text, *chia* is followed by *jên*, "man, men." Some other interpreters have in one way or another bent the meaning of *chia* in order to connect it to *jên*, but none of the resulting statements that I've read have made sense to me in context. Noticing that the *jên* in question is followed in the text by another *jên* that begins the next sentence (which I eventually moved), I theorized that a copyist mistakenly wrote the character twice. So I eliminated it from the text of line six, which produced a line that fit with the one before it.

Following the text of that sixth line was a question that I for reasons given below eventually preceded with something else (lines seven and eight). That question was *jên chih pu shan ho ch'i chih yu*, which I translated as:

> man/men it/its/him/his/them/their/these/those not good why?
> abandon/discard/reject it/its/him/his/them/their/these/those have/
> possess/exist

My first interpretation was:

> Those not-good men [–] why [have they] abandoned/discarded/rejected them [sweet words, respectful conduct] possess/exist?

Aside from the presence of *yu* ("have, possess," "exist"), which seemed as out-of-place as a dog in a flower garden, what bothered me about that interpretation was something that the author appears to have been quite aware of, namely that the bad have *not* abandoned, discarded, or rejected sweet words and respectful conduct. As has been true probably since the start of the human race, a great many bad people employ sweet words and respectful conduct to fool potential victims and acquire what they want. Elsewhere in the *Way Virtue Classic*, the author recommends that seekers go beyond Confucian words and conduct to deeper matters—so why would he be concerned here about the bad abandoning or rejecting such words and conduct?

Another possible interpretation of the characters, I considered, would be:

Those not-good men [–] why abandon them possess/exist?

But with that interpretation, even leaving out "possess/exist," there was no continuity. To go from "Sweet words can buy and sell, respectful conduct can add to them" to something like "Why abandon the bad?" would be disjointed (as other interpretations of that part of the text tend to be).

Then I tried the definitions "it" and "its" for *chih*—which, despite the still-puzzling final character, produced a much more promising question:

Those not-good men [–] why [have they] abandoned/discarded/rejected it/its possess/exist?

Believing by then that something preceding the characters of the above had been left out of the text, I went back to "Sweet words can buy and sell, respectful conduct can add to them," and to supply continuity wrote after that "But those do not redeem the bad—only The Way can do that."

Then I turned to the puzzle of *yu* ("have, possess," "exist"). The interpretations I consulted had left it out as something that didn't belong. Undoubtedly, I thought, it didn't—but maybe something else did.

I looked up other *yus* in the analytical dictionaries and saw a closely related character: *yu*, "aid, assist," "urge," "stimulate." *Yu*, "have, possess," "exist," consists of a right hand over the moon. (In ancient times, it depicted a right hand over a bundle of dried meat—the latter of which was almost identical to, and was later mistaken for, the ancient character for "moon.") *Yu*, "aid," assist," "urge," "stimulate," consists of a right hand over the moon (originally meat) joined by a compressed version of the two-stroke character for "man." I suspected that a sloppy copyist left out the "man," thereby leaving us with "have, possess," "exist." Plugging in the most likely definition of the second *yu*, I came up with:

Those not-good men [–] why [have they] rejected its assistance?

Which became "So why have the bad rejected its assistance?"

The second stanza apparently refers to how a prince would present himself and pay his respects during special ceremonies of state at the palace of "the Son of Heaven," the Chou Dynasty's king. Lines seven and eight, "Even though your hands are filled / With a tablet disc of jade," are my interpretation of *sui yu kung pi*, "although have both hands jade disc." *Kung pi*, according to Dr. Yi Wu's notes on the chapter, means "to hold (or encircle) jade with two hands." A *pi* in this chapter's context, according to James Legge, was a prince's "round symbol of rank large enough to fill both the hands." Lines eight and nine, "And your carriage is to be pulled / By a splendid four-horse team," are my version of the text's *i hsien ssu ma*, "with preceding team-of-four horses"—in simpler English, "with before you a four-horse team." In his chapter notes, Dr. Yi Wu writes that "A four-horse team indicates a powerful person's luxurious carriage. As with jade items, examples have been found in recently excavated tombs of high ranked nobles." All of which would seem to indicate that the author was familiar with the arrival procedure for a prince on such occasions.

"Ancient" in the stanza's final line is my in-that-context interpretation of *tz'ŭ*, which originally meant "stop and turn" in this case, I believe, meaning "looking back," "the former," or "the past"—but which now means "this." Other interpreters of the chapter either use "this" ("this Way") or seemingly ignore the character. "Ancient" was an easy word choice when I considered the text of the next stanza's first sentence, which includes *ku*, "the ancients," "those of old," which I rendered as "the ancestors."

In translation, the text of my third stanza's lines three through seven reads: "[Is it] not said accordingly [that those who] seek obtain [and that those who] have transgressions accordingly [are] forgiven?"

On a more personal note: There are many chapters of the *Way Virtue Classic* that I'm particularly fond of. If I were to make a list of them, it would be a long one. But of them all, this one is my favorite.

63.

DO WITHOUT DOING

It follows from the whole chapter that the Taoistic "doing nothing" was not an absolute quiescence and inaction, but had a method in it.
JAMES LEGGE

The above quotation from James Legge's notes on Chapter Sixty-Three sums up the chapter's contents nicely: The author gives away some secrets of his *wei wu wei*, "doing without doing."

The text of my first stanza's first three lines is *wei wu wei shih wu shih wei wu wei*, which I translated as "Do without doing, work without working, taste without tasting." However, the second *wei*, "taste" or "savor," made no sense to me in context. Suspecting that a copyist had somehow confused one character with another, I searched for look-alike characters but found nothing promising. Then I searched for sound-alike characters and found *wei*, "speak," "say." When I considered the author's anti-Confucianist, "stop the sweet words and busyness" attitude expressed in various other chapters, "speak" made a good deal of sense. Preferring a character that made sense to one that did not, I replaced "taste" and "tasting" with "talk" and "talking," which has the author saying "Do without forcing, work without struggling, talk without flattery-chattering and word-wasting."

Regarding the first stanza's last line, "Repay ill will with Virtue": Repaying ill will with ill will makes a situation more difficult for all concerned, which is not in line with *wu wei*.

Two statements in Chapter Sixty-Three are so cryptic that they must be added to in order to make them understandable:

Concerning the first: The text of my first stanza's lines four and five is *ta hsiao to shao*, "large small many few," which I interpreted in context as "Make the large small; make the many few." Some other interpretations I've seen say the opposite: "Enlarge the small, increase the few," which to me hardly fits the theme of *making work easier and simpler*. I believe the author is saying: Reduce intimidating and complicated matters to their basic components or principles—*the small* and *the few*—then operate from them in order to avoid struggle.

Concerning the second cryptic statement: The text of my fourth stanza's lines three and four is *to i pi to nan*, "much/more easy must much/more difficult," which I interpreted in context as "What they see as very easy proves much more difficult."

In line one of the fourth stanza, "those who promise lightly"—*fu ch'ing nê*, "those [who] lightly assent/commit/promise"—are the overoptimistic and overconfident, who do not carefully observe a situation before committing themselves.

In the same stanza, I added the words that make up lines seven and eight ("So they begin with the easiest and smallest parts of it") to clarify what the text of my lines five, six, nine, and ten seems to be saying: "Therefore wise man [treats] as difficult it" (my version: "The wise, however, treat work as difficult") and "So to the last without difficulty" (my version: "And to the end, they have no difficulty").

64.

BEGINNINGS

Regarding "split" in the third line of my first stanza: The text's *p'an* is defined as "the semicircular pool before the provincial colleges of old, "a college," "a graduate," "Confucian temple." I looked through the characters listed under *p'an* and found the most likely one for the context: *p'an*, "cleave," "separate," "to halve." The text's *p'an*, "semicircular pool," consists of "water" plus "half"; *p'an*, "cleave," consists of "knife" plus "half." Another text I checked used the latter character. Other interpretations present *p'an* in this chapter as "shatter."

San, the last character in the text of line four, is typically interpreted as "scatter." The original character (different from the brush-character *san*) meant "to break hemp," and therefore "to break up," "to break."

"A minute grain of pollen" in my second stanza's second line is my interpretation of *hao* ("infinitesimally small") *mo* ("end of a branch," "powder," "dust"), the combination of which is interpreted in other editions as "small shoot," "tiny sprout," and such. By the definitions, *mo* means to me the typically very small, short-lived male conifer cones at the tips of branchlets, and the dust-like pollen they release.

The text of my next two lines is *chiu* ("nine") *ts'êng* ("story," "level") *chih* (possessive sign) *t'ai* ("tower") *ch'i* ("rise[s]") *yü* ("on") *lei* (now defined as "to tie, to bind," "to connect") *t'u* ("earth, ground, soil"). The ancient definition of *lei*, however—with a partially different pictograph—was "three articles connected or tied together." The sentence seemed to be missing a couple of characters. When I considered that a traditional Chinese tower is built of stones, bricks, and wood, "three stones joined on the ground" became my interpretation of *lei t'u*.

The stanza's last two lines, "A three-hundred-mile journey / Starts on what is under one's foot," are from *ch'ien* ("thousand") *li* (approximately one-third mile) *chih* (possessive sign) *hsing* ("walk," "travel") *shih* ("begins") *yü* ("on") *tsu* ("foot") *hsia* ("under").

In my final stanza, I modified "desire not desire/long for" (*yü pu yü*) into "desire *beyond-desiring*" (line one) and modified "learn not learn/study" (*hsüeh pu hsüeh*) into "learn *beyond-studying*" (line four). After I'd taken into account the author's frequently expressed *wei wu wei* attitude, as in the previous chapter and in this related chapter's third stanza and ending statement, I concluded that "desire not desire" means "desire *not-desire*"—that the wise get rid of desires not by struggling against them (by desiring *not to desire*) but by looking beyond them to a better state, that of *freedom from them*, the state of *not-desire*. And by "learn not learn," I concluded that the author means that the wise go beyond *taught* learning—*studying*, the way of learning that they acquired from others, especially that advocated by the Confucians (study, study more, study harder)–to the state of *not-study*, the natural, childlike, pre-taught learning that many have lost. The wise "return to what the many have left behind." They go beyond merely *acquiring secondhand information* to *acquiring firsthand knowledge and wisdom.*

Other translations/interpretations of the characters of the two final lines of my last stanza, *erh pu kan wei*, tend toward "Thus they do not dare to act," or some equivalent. My basic translation, "Thus [they do] not violently act," interpreted the third character, *kan*, pictographically–not as the traditional interpretation's "daring" or "boldness" but as "violence," as I did in Chapter Thirty and as I explain in my notes for Chapter Seventy-Three. "Not dare to act" and the like simply didn't fit.

"Inner light" in my final stanza's seventh line is my in-context interpretation of *tzŭ* ("self") *jan* ("to light," "thus," "so"), a phrase usually interpreted throughout the *Tao Te Ching* and in writings on Taoism as "self-so," "spontaneous, spontaneity," "[one's] own nature," or "inner nature." *Tzŭ jan* could be pictographically, literally translated as "self-lighting," "self light" ("self's light"), or "self-burning." In this case, I liked the image of "self light," which I interpreted as *inner light*–something that could be extinguished by harsh or insensitive treatment.

65.

SIMPLICITY

In Chapter Sixty-Five, the author contrasts cleverness with simplicity. The cleverness appears to be the "What's in it for me?" kind–which, indicates the author, infects rulers and subjects alike, weakening the state. A "What's in it for me?" ruler, he implies, creates a "What's in it for me?" society. The wise ruler, he says, knows to turn away from that selfish cleverness to selfless simplicity. And that simplicity produces a well-behaved society, not one of trickiness and greed.

The chapter's text starts with *ku*, "the ancients." I interpreted that as "the rulers of ancient times," as they clearly are the ones being referred to.

In my first stanza, I shifted the text's emphasis from *fei*, "*not*," to *ming*, "to enlighten," in the third line and added emphasis to the following line.

"Growing" in the fifth line is one of the ancient meanings of *chih*, "grow, develop," "continue, progress."

"Clever" in the first stanza and "cleverness" in the second are my interpretations of another *chih*, which, depending on the context, means "knowledge," "cleverness," or "wisdom." Other interpretations of the chapter tend to present it as "knowledge"– thereby saying, as do interpretations of Chapter Three, that a good ruler makes sure that his people are without knowledge. But the simplicity that the author frequently advocates for the wise, for rulers, and for subjects is not a state of ignorance, any more than his "doing without doing" is what a good many people in Chinese history (the Confucianists, the Communists) have said it is—laziness.

In my fourth stanza, second line, "all" is my in-that-context interpretation of *wu*, "things," which can sometimes mean "people generally" or "situations." In the same line, I added "to simplicity" for clarity.

The fourth stanza's final word, "cooperation," is my interpretation of *shun*, "to follow," "to obey," "pliant," "docile," "easy."

Almost all of the translations/interpretations that I've seen of Chapter Sixty-Five show the same sort of insensitivity to the author's intentions that I see in translations/interpretations of Chapter Three. The following is a refreshing exception to the rule. Although it's not as faithful to certain characters as I have attempted to be, it's far more faithful than others tend to be. From the book *Lao Tzu: Tao Teh Ching, Translated by John C. H. Wu* (St. John's University Press, New York, 1961):

> In the old days, those who were well versed in the practice of the Tao did not try to enlighten the people, but rather to keep them in the state of simplicity. For, why are the people hard to govern? Because they are too clever! Therefore, he who governs his state with cleverness is its malefactor, but he who governs his state without resorting to cleverness is its benefactor. To know these principles is to possess a rule and a measure. To keep the rule and the measure constantly in your mind is what we call Mystical Virtue. Deep and far-reaching is Mystical Virtue! It leads all things to return, till they come back to Great Harmony!

66.
RULERS OF THE HUNDRED VALLEYS

The power of *yin*: dismissed as impractical by a great many, applied to impressive advantage by a relative few. We all know the names of some of those who've made use of it; but the majority of names we will probably never know. It's usually their opposites that we're made aware of—those of arrogance, selfishness, and violence. They, and those who present their behavior as heroic, exciting, or admirable, poison our society and our world.

In Chapter Sixty-Six, large bodies of water fed by their tributaries are compared to rulers, who receive the tributes of their subjects. Such bodies of water produce their own microclimates—major rivers and lakes thereby to a great extent "control" the valleys that contain them, and can therefore be said to rule the valleys. If they were to dry up, the valleys would die.

In a similar manner, the rulers of humanity produce their own "microclimates," whether of integrity, dynamic energy, and inspiration or of cruelty, egotism, and cunning. If they want to maintain their leadership positions over time, they need to be for the people, not for themselves. Like the great rivers and lakes, which keep their territories alive and healthy by attracting and releasing moisture from below, they need to rule with humility, not with arrogance. Otherwise, those whom they rule will despise them and possibly—as history has shown—depose them.

The two characters that make up the text of line one of my first stanza are *chiang*, "large river[s]," and *hai*, "sea," "arm[s] of the ocean," "lake[s]," "expanse[s]." I interpreted *hai* as "expansive lakes," because that seemed to best fit the "hundred valleys' rulers" (*pai ku wang*) context. Other interpretations I've seen use "sea" or "seas," "ocean" or "oceans."

"Rulers" in the second line of my first stanza is my interpretation of the text's *wang*, "king," "ruler," "royal."

In the text of the first line of my second stanza, I interpreted *yü shang min*, "desire [to be] above the people," as "want to rule the people."

In the text of the stanza's third line, I interpreted *yü hsien min,* "desire [to be] first/ahead/before the people," as "want to lead the people."

In the text of the second and third lines of my third stanza, I interpreted *ch'u shang*, "dwell[s] /settle[s] down above," as "eventually comes to rest in a high position" because, as one analytical dictionary elaborated on *ch'u*, "The primitive idea of this [character] was to have walked until tired, *chih*, and come to a seat, *chi*."

In the stanza's fifth and sixth lines, "eventually comes to rest in an advanced position" is from *ch'u ch'ien,* "dwell[s] / settle[s] down advance[d]."

I interpreted *hai*, "hurt," "injure[d]," in the text of my third stanza's seventh line as "feel slighted."

The text of my fourth stanza—*i ch'i pu chêng ku t'ien hsia mo nêng yü chih chêng*, "Because he [does] not contend, so [superfluous character] under heaven [is] not able to give him contention"—is almost identical to a statement in Chapter Twenty-Two. It seemed to fit just as well in this chapter as in the other.

67.
THREE TREASURES

Although the first part of this chapter has been interpreted in a variety of ways, I believe that I can sum up most of the existing English-language interpretations I've seen as:

"Under heaven, everyone says that my Way is great, and [or "but"] seems unlike everything else. But it is precisely because it is unlike everything else that it is able to be great. If it were like everything else, it would for a long time now have been small."

That beginning section of the chapter, in the interpretations I've read, has always bothered me—but I didn't know why. Now I know why:

Other interpretations of the introductory sentences heavily imply that the author is well known in the world of his time, and that his doctrine of The Way, his way of The Way, is considered great by everyone. Yet elsewhere the author says that he is misperceived and underestimated by others (Chapter Twenty) and that no one can know or practice his words, his principles (Chapter Seventy). All interpretations I've read of the first part of this chapter contradict as well the apparent historical reality that I mentioned in my introduction—namely that the author by all appearances had no followers, and that his true identity was apparently completely unknown.

I need to mention that some Chinese texts of the *Tao Te Ching* (but not the standard Wang Pi text) leave the character *tao* out of the chapter's beginning, thereby having the author say, in some English-language interpretations, "Under heaven, everyone says that I am great, and unlike everyone else. But it is precisely because I am unlike everyone else that I am able to be great." And more than a bit egotistical, it would seem.

For the above reasons, I was prepared to declare in these notes that at least the first part of the chapter seemed fraudulent—that it appeared to have been written by someone who'd been taken in by the "Master Lao" legend and had somehow missed or misunderstood what the author says in Chapter Twenty and Chapter Seventy. But then I investigated the ancestors of the characters in the text of my first stanza, and changed my mind. I concluded that research by thinking: *It's no wonder he didn't want his identity known.*

The characters in the text of my first stanza are:

t'ien ("heaven") *hsia* ("under") *chieh* ("all") *wei* ("say") *wo* ("I," "my") *tao* ("way," "Way") *ta* ("great," "noble," "eminent" "foremost," "best"—in other words, *worthy of esteem*) *ssu* ("seem[s]") *pu* ("not") *hsiao* (now meaning "like," "resembling," "to reproduce")

fu ("man," "it," "the one in question") *wei* ("namely") *ta* ("great," etc.)
ku ("because") *ssu* ("seem[s] ") *pu* ("not") *hsiao* (now meaning "like," etc.)

jo ("if") *hsiao* (now meaning "like," etc.) *chiu* ("long time") *i* (emphasis character) *ch'i* ("it") *hsi* ("small") *yeh fu* (emphasis/final particles)

With any of those definitions of *hsiao* (now meaning "like," "resembling," "to reproduce") an interpreter would need to do what other interpreters of this chapter have done—

follow the translation of that character with "everything else," "anything else," "everyone else's," or "anyone else's," in order to produce a coherent statement: "Under heaven, everyone says that my Way [or "way"] is great, and seems not like anyone else's." But, I discovered, the ancient-character meaning of *hsiao* was not "like" but "like one's father." (As one source tritely put it, "a chip off the old block.") So the author means that his Way, or way, is *not like his father's.*

Taking into consideration the "new" context established by *hsiao*'s ancient meaning, I interpreted *tao* in the text of my second line not as "Way" but as "way"—one's personal path, philosophy, or behavior. And I interpreted *ta* ("great," "noble," "eminent," "foremost," "best") as "noble." Doing so and applying the "like one's father" definition of *hsiao* made sensible as well the passage as given in the above-mentioned *tao*-less texts: "Under heaven, everyone says that I am noble—I seem not like my father."

While working on the stanza, I began to wonder if what eventually became known as the *Tao Te Ching* had been a diary or private journal.

I read the lines of Chapter Fifty-Three again: "The Great Way is very easy, but the family is fond of the shortest path. The royal court is neglected. The fields are full of weeds. The granaries are empty." I recalled the author's frequent, seemingly accustomed use of characters such as *hou*, "prince," and his prince-centered analogies and examples: "Even though your hands are filled with a tablet disc of jade" (Chapter Sixty-Two); "Therefore, the wise prince, when traveling all day, does not go far from his baggage-wagons" (Chapter Twenty-Six).

The author, I thought, was the son of a prince. His father was a "lord of ten thousand warrior-wagons" (Chapter Twenty-Six). And they likely lived in or near the central plains: "Where soldiers have encamped, thorns and brambles grow. When a large army passes, a lean year surely follows" (Chapter Thirty).

For 2,400 years or so, I reflected, the inquisitive have attempted to learn the indisputable identity of "Master Lao," the alleged older contemporary of Confucius. But the "Old Master" has proved untraceable, as if he had never existed—because, it now would seem, he never had. The inquisitive have been looking for the wrong man, so it's not surprising that they haven't found the right one. Maybe, I thought, he could finally be found—in a royal tomb, I imagined—and long-overdue credit could be given to him.

While going over the characters of this chapter, I managed to put aside my previous impressions of what they are saying, impressions created by the many translations/interpretations I'd read. Only then could I see that Chapter Sixty-Seven is the author's criticism of his "rob-and-boasters" clan and of others like them, and an expression of his own very different beliefs.

Consider the character *kuang*, commonly translated (or mis-translated) in this chapter as "generous" and "generosity," which I present as "expansive" in my third stanza's second line and as "great expansion" in my fourth stanza's fourth line. *Kuang* means "expansive, expand," "broad, broaden," "enlarged, enlarge," "vast." The character shows a roof over "yellow," the color of heaven, of the halls of "the Son of Heaven," and of China's loessial terrain—all large, expansive, and vast. In the text of my fourth stanza, the author is therefore not, as previous interpretations have it, criticizing those who are *wastefully generous*; he's implying that his father and clan, their soldiers, and others like them are *aggressively, ruthlessly ambitious for expansion.*

A final translation note: The text of the last line of my third stanza, *nêng ch'êng ch'i chang*, translates as "can become utensils' senior chief," the individual in charge of the royal ceremonial utensils. But, as I explain in my notes for Chapter Twenty-Eight, *ch'i*, "utensils," was ancient slang for governmental lackeys, technical specialists, soldiers, and low-ranking employees. So "senior chief of utensils" in this case would be slang for "leader of lower-ranking men" or "leader of soldiers."

By the time I'd finished this chapter, my mental "picture" of the author was fairly clear. But as it turned out, more clarifying elements were waiting a few chapters further on.

68.
NOT CONTENDING

In my first stanza, first line, "manager of men" is my interpretation of *shih*, defined as "scholar," "gentleman," or "officer" (military or civil). *Shih* consists of the number ten above the number one, signifying, say the analytical dictionaries, *everything from one to ten* (ten being a complete unit in the Chinese counting system) and therefore signifying *someone who knows all things*. Other interpretations of this chapter present *shih* as "soldier," "warrior," or "officer," However:

According to the *Shuo Wên* (described in "Ancient Pictures, Ghostly Voices"), this *shih* is related by origin to *shih*, "to serve," "affairs," "business," "[government] office," or "matters." According to the analytical classical dictionaries I consulted, this chapter's *shih* represents "a manager of affairs" (said one dictionary) and (according to another) "by extension, a sage, a man pointed out by his learning to become an official." So I interpreted the character by those definitions as "manager of men."

In the second line of my first stanza, "fighter" is from *chan*, "to fight." The principle stated, "A skilled fighter is not angry," applies to more than warfare. In the martial arts, for example, anger throws one's timing off. It causes a fighter to take foolish chances by concentrating on offense and ignoring defense, leaving unguarded areas that even a beginner could attack. It adds stress to an already stressful situation, and quickly tires one out.

In the first stanza's third and fourth lines, going by what seemed the chapter's context—one broader than the usual interpretation would tend to indicate—I interpreted *ti*, "an enemy," "a competitor," "to oppose," as "opposition" and interpreted *yü*, "join," "together with," "associate with," as "become entangled with it."

Regarding the statements of the second stanza: The Way does not contend. It operates instead by modesty, cooperation, and effortlessness. So emulating The Way—practicing what the author refers to elsewhere as "the way of the wise"—is, says the text, *ku chih chi*, "[the] ancient ones' ultimate."

69.
CAUTION

The first two characters in the text of my first stanza are *yung* ("to use, employ") *ping* ("soldier," "military," "weapons"). Regarding *yung*: As I did in Chapter Four (and as explained in the notes for that chapter), I concluded that someone misread the almost-identical ancient ancestor of *chung* as *yung*. The second of the two listed ways of intonating *chung* is defined as "accomplish, accomplished," "to hit"—referring to the ability of a skilled archer to hit the center (*chung*) of a target. "Accomplished soldiers" seemed to me a more likely wording than "employed soldiers," "[those who] employ soldiers," or "[those who] use weapons," especially considering that *chê*, "those who," does not appear in the text. I ended up replacing "soldiers" with the more generic "fighters," as I believe the principles expressed are applicable to more than military strategy.

In the third line, "master" (*chu*) in this case means "master of the house"—the host who hurries forward to greet his guests, who modestly pull back.

In *The Book of Lao Tzu*, Dr. Yi Wu has this to say about the text of my first stanza:

> One who advances is exposed; retreat protects one's power to take advantage of an opponent's rashness. This is called "advancing by retreating."

The strategy of stepping back is also a matter of drawing one's opponent in, giving him a misleading sense of superiority that will make him negligent and vulnerable—*yin*, pulling back, lures aggressive *yang*. (American Indian warriors used this tactic to great advantage when defending their territories.) At the same time, it enables one to study the opponent's character and tendencies.

The second stanza's text colorfully points out that the above *yin* strategy is also a *wu wei* strategy: Without "doing" anything, it puts pressure on the opponent to make the first move, and thereby sets him up to make the first mistakes. "Pushing without opposing" (line four) is my possibly unique interpretation of *jêng* ("drag along," "push," "throw," "fling away") *wu* ("without") *ti* ("enemy," "competitor," "to oppose"). Interpretations in other editions vary widely in meaning. "Pushing without opposing" would mean "putting pressure on the opponent by taking a *yin* position."

Although the wording of my second stanza differs considerably from that of the other interpretations I've seen, it follows the characters of the text. I don't know what the other versions I've seen are based on, but they don't appear to be based on the characters of the standard text.

The typical interpretation of the text of my third stanza's first three lines goes something like: "There is no calamity greater than underestimating the enemy." "Underestimating the enemy" is from *ch'ing* ("light," "frivolous," "easy," "think lightly of") *ti* ("enemy," "competitor," "to oppose"). Looking at the "big picture" of what the author seems to be saying, and consequently choosing "think lightly of" and "to oppose," I came up with what seemed in context an interpretation more fitting than the usual: "No calamity is greater than the results of thinking lightly of battle." The only one like it that I found in a quick search of other versions is that by James Legge: "There is no calamity greater than lightly engaging in war."

"Inflict violence" in my fourth stanza is my in-that-context interpretation of *chia*, "to add to," "to increase," "to inflict." *Chia* consists of *k'ou*, "mouth," plus *li*, "muscle." One meaning of the character, said an analytical dictionary, would be: "To add muscle to persuasion, [inflict] violence."

The text of the last two lines of my fourth stanza is *ai* ("grieve for," "sorry," "sad") *chê* ("one who," "those who," "that which") *shêng* ("conquer," "excel," "outdo"). The statement is interpreted in other editions as "He who deplores the situation conquers," "It's the one who feels grief that will win," "Victory belongs to the grieving side," and so on. Going by those interpretations, I didn't understand what was being said. Why would the side that feels sorry or sad win the confrontation? Why was that side grieving–because it had to fight? Because the situation had degenerated into armed conflict? I'm not aware of any recorded situation in which the grieving side won a battle. Did someone leave out an explanatory character after *ai*?

I put the chapter away for days to clear my mind of the fourth stanza's text. When I finally looked at the chapter again, I noticed the interpretation I'd arrived at of the text of the previous stanza's last three lines: "Thinking lightly of battle brings us closer to losing what we value." The last four words made me again consider the possibility of a character having been left out after *ai* in *ai chê shêng*, "sorry / one who / outdo." I came up with three possible characters: *k'uei*, "to fail," "to lose," "to be deficient"; *sang*, "to die, to perish," "to lose"; and *shu*, "to lose," "ruined." Only with the inclusion of such a character could I make sense of the statement. The result was: "The side that would be sorrier to lose will prevail."

I once got into a conversation about the *Tao Te Ching* with my first Chinese *T'ai Chi Ch'üan* teacher, David Cheng, who had grown up in a Taoist monastery in Taiwan after escaping from the People's Republic. "Everybody talks about the *Tao Te Ching* as *spiritual*," he told me, "but it's a good deal more than that. Notice how much of it is about the workings of politics and warfare—*from an insider's point of view*. The man who wrote those verses was more than a philosopher. His comments on politics and warfare carry weight because he knew by experience of some sort what they were about." While working on this chapter, I remembered those words, and realized that they had planted an idea in my mind that eventually led to my conclusions—as given in my notes for Chapter Sixty-Seven, and as given in my notes for the next chapter—about the author of the *Tao Te Ching*.

70.
MY WORDS

Returning to the thought I mentioned in my notes for Chapter Sixty-Seven, namely that what eventually became known as the *Tao Te Ching* might have been some sort of diary: Chapter Seventy seems to me to be a classic, quintessential diary entry. So in its own quirky way does the other autobiographical chapter, Chapter Twenty. Other chapters—especially Ten, Sixteen, Forty-Two, Forty-Nine, Fifty-Three, and Sixty-Seven—contain autobiographical elements. Even the non-autobiographical chapters could be seen as the kinds of reflections, theories, observations, and ideas that someone of genius might have recorded in a diary. All of which could explain, among other things, the author's sometimes-sketchy, often-abbreviated wording.

The following stanza-by-stanza explanation of what I've concluded the author is saying in this chapter not only differs significantly from any I've read, it differs significantly from what I not long ago believed to be true.

In the text of my first stanza, rather than bitterly complaining about the inability of all of those "under heaven" *to understand* his words (the long-accepted interpretation), the author is, I believe, expressing sadness and frustration at not being in a position *to communicate* his words to those out in the world, as a result of which society cannot know of them and cannot put them into practice—*t'ien hsia mo nêng chih mo nêng hsing*, "Under heaven, none can know [them]; none can walk/perform [them]." In Chapter Forty-Two he seems to indicate, as my notes on that chapter point out, that he intends to or wants to teach. But, he indicates in this chapter, someone or something is preventing him from realizing his ambition.

In the text of my second stanza, he says that words have "ancestors" (*tsung*), by which I believe he means that words have origins or causes, such as experiences, observations, and thoughts. He next says, in my interpretation, that writers (*shih*) have "sovereigns" (*chün*)—superiors of one sort or another to whom they must give allegiance. (An explanation of my interpretation of *shih* as "writers" follows shortly.) He then says that "men" (*fu*)—others beyond his social circle—do not know his word-ancestors and sovereigns, and accordingly do not know *him*. (I strongly suspect that his family, though they are close to him and are most likely the sovereigns he refers to, also do not know him—or his philosophy.)

In the text of my third stanza, the author seems to say that since those out "under heaven" cannot know him, and since most of those around him neither know about nor care about his ideas or philosophy-teaching ambitions, he is doing what he can under such isolating circumstances: *write*. But, since those who "rule" (*tsai*) him are "honored" (*kuei*)—powerful and influential enough to stop his plans—he is writing secretly, in disguise: "So, to resemble a wise man, I put on coarse cloth and conceal the jade." (Explanations of my interpretation-choices "rule" and "to resemble" follow shortly.) The "jade" (*yü*) that he's concealing (*huai*, "enfold in one's garments") symbolizes his royal origins. As for the "coarse cloth" (*ho*) disguise he's putting on:

My theory of the origin of the legendary Lao-tzŭ, the "Old Master," is that the author labeled his diary something like the Chinese equivalent of *Thoughts of the Old Master*, to hide its true authorship from the eyes of his family and clan—and to help ensure that none of them would read it—until he could set out on his own, away from their powerful, dominating influence. Far from writing his thoughts down for others as the Lao-tzŭ legend maintains, he was writing them down *for himself*, intending for at least some of them to be used later, when he became a teacher of philosophy.

But, I wondered, if his recorded thoughts had been so private, why and how did they come to be released to the public? And why did someone with such wise, penetrating vision not eventually become a popular, revered teacher of philosophy and a well-documented opponent of Master K'ung's system? An answer to those questions came to me in a strange way:

While finishing work on this chapter, I received the strong impression that its author had died at a young age, shortly after completing his writing—which therefore may not have been as complete as it otherwise would have been. I don't know where that impression came from—it seemed to have nothing to do with what I'd by then deduced about the author from his wording; it seemed to have no apparent connection to the characters-analyzing and the maze-walking. But it kept corning back to me, and I found that I couldn't dispel it. It was an impression accompanied by deep sadness.

Regarding my likely unique interpretation of the character *shih* in this chapter's context as "writers" (second stanza, second line): Classical dictionary definitions of *shih* are "affairs," "business," "[government] office," and "matters," none of which seemed to me to fit the chapter's context any more than do the interpretations "deeds" or "actions" found in the usual presentations. *Shih* consists of the symbol for "he," "she," "they," or "it" above the depiction of a hand holding a writing tube. That could signify *clerk* (business), *scribe* (office), or *writer* (affairs, matters). Unlike any of the other characters for "write" (such as *shu*, which contains a hand holding a writing tube), *shih* pictographically shows *someone* using the device—a writer. I suspect, therefore, that "writer" was once one of *shih*'s primary meanings, if not *the* primary meaning. Whether or not that's true, "writers" seemed the interpretation most appropriate to the context—and, considering the author's pictographic tendencies, therefore the most likely intended meaning.

Regarding my likely unique "those who rule me" (third stanza, second line): In my beginning translation, except for the key character I left for last, the text of the first two lines of my third stanza said:

know me those who few *tsai* me those who honored

Or, filled out and in English-language word order:

Those who know me [are] few; those who *tsai* me [are] honored.

The analytical dictionary definitions of *tsai* (also spelled *tsê*) are: "law, rule," "pattern, model," "according to," "in that way," "thus," "consequently," "then," "thereupon." I chose the verb form of "rule," the only likely choice.

A typical interpretation of the text of the above translation goes something like: "Since those who know me are few, then I am of value." Another popular version: "Those who know me are few, so those who follow me are valued." The first interpretation doesn't conform to the characters, and doesn't make sense. The second interpretation isn't true to any definition of *tsai*. And its implication that the author has followers contradicts historical reality as well as what he says about his words—that under heaven, no one can know and practice them.

Regarding "to resemble a wise man": As it exists today, the text of the chapter's final statement, *shih i shêng jên pei ho huai yü*, translates as:

therefore ["thus accordingly," "rightly and accordingly"] wise man
    covers/wraps/puts on [not "wears," the traditional translation]
coarse cloth enfolds jade

The traditional interpretation is:

Therefore the sage wears coarse clothing and enfolds the jade.

From this writer's point of view, that interpretation of the text, as the text exists today, produces a weak ending and an inconsistent composition. Having deciphered the *Way Virtue Classic* using the ancient-character meanings—not merely those of the brush characters, which frequently muddle passages—I would say that the author had definitely mastered the skills of composition. Would a skilled composition-writer, having started out with "My words" (first stanza), having continued with "know me" (second stanza), and having gone on to "know me" and "rule me" (third stanza) then conclude his strong, first-person composition by lamely and impersonally stating "Therefore the sage wears coarse clothing and enfolds the jade"? What does a generic wise man wearing coarse clothing and concealing jade have to do with "Those who know me are few; those who rule me are honored"? Where is the personal connection? What is the relevance to the rest of the chapter?

Apparently in an effort to relate the generic-wise-man statement to what precedes it, some scholars and interpreters have claimed or implied in their commentaries that "the sage" is Master Lao's reference *to himself*, and that the "jade" he's concealing in his coarse-cloth attire symbolizes philosophical truths, Virtue, or wisdom, depending on the individual scholar's or interpreter's opinion. However, "the sage" could not be Master Lao, because—as I believe the clues in previous chapters have revealed—there is no Master Lao. And for the author to call *himself* a wise man, or to even imply that he is one, would be un-Chinese and very out-of-character. And again: *pei* does not mean "wear," it means "to cover," "to wrap," "to put on." Its "picture" consists of "blanket" plus "to cover." As for *yü*, "jade":

Faced with a choice between "jade" as symbolizing philosophical truths, etc. or as symbolizing the author's royal status, I considered the clues that previous chapters had provided regarding the author's social standing, the statements he makes in this chapter, and the fact that the *Tao Te Ching*'s other references to jade (in Chapter Nine and Chapter Thirty-Nine) treat it not as supposed truths, etc. but as what it indisputably was—the stone of aristocrats and the ultimate status symbol of ancient China. After I'd considered all that, the most likely significance of "jade" in this chapter's context seemed obvious. What seemed equally obvious in context was that the author in the chapter's concluding statement should both logically and compositionally be saying: "Therefore, to resemble a wise man, I put on coarse cloth [as "Master Lao"] and enfold the jade."

My theory about the origin of the text's incongruous ending-statement is that a very early copyist, acting from the assumption that the author was in truth a philosophical master syled Lao-tzŭ, "Old Master," eliminated as a mistake a character such as *jo* or *ju*, "to resemble," "to be like," following *shih i*, "thus accordingly," "therefore," and eliminated as another mistake a *wo*, "I," following *shêng jên*, "wise man," thereby changing "Therefore, to resemble wise man, I put on coarse cloth, enfold jade" to "Therefore wise man puts on coarse cloth, enfolds jade."

In the final analysis, I believe, the determination of what the author is saying in this chapter or any other comes down to this simple principle:

The "Ariadne's thread" that can enable one to work through the treacherous, exasperating labyrinth known as the *Tao Te Ching* and return with understandable statements consists of five words: *Writing needs to make sense.*

71.
TO KNOW

The shorter and simpler a *Tao Te Ching* chapter appears, the more difficult to decipher it can be, because there's less context to go by. My translated text of this chapter can demonstrate what I mean:

> know/knowing not know/knowing above/superior/high
> not know/knowing know/knowing sickness/defect/fault
> man/men only sickness/defect/fault sickness/defect/fault
> is/are/thus accordingly not sickness/defect/fault
> wise man/men not sickness/defect/fault
> because he/they sickness/defect/fault sickness/defect/fault
> is/are/thus accordingly not sickness/defect/fault

My first impression of the above was that some characters had been left out. My second impression was that *one* had been left out–*chih*, "know" or "knowing"–after the first character in the third line and the second character in the sixth line. The author, I thought, is playing a minimalist word game, using as few characters as possible to say something. My third impression was that someone else added the last three lines, which to me seemed redundant, stating as they do, through rewording, some of what already has been said and then repeating part of a previous statement. So I left those lines–my version of which I'll give further on–out of my interpretation.

The first two lines of the above can be, and have been, interpreted in many ways. A reasonable, though wordy, possibility would be: "To know that we do not know–to recognize the limitations of our knowledge–is superior knowledge. To not know that we know–to fail to realize when, or that, we know something–is faulty knowledge." But is that what was meant?

After coming up with three or four wordy, explanatory interpretations like the above, I decided to attempt a more literal, minimalist one, choosing "defect" as the most appropriate definition, in context, of *ping*, "sickness" "defect," or "fault." What helped me the most was my awareness of the author's tendencies, in particular his fondness for setting up pairs of contrasting terms. From the latter I concluded that "know/knowing not know/knowing" meant "to know *not-knowing*," and that "not know/knowing know/knowing" meant "to not know *knowing*."

In the context of this playing-with-words chapter ("know not know" versus "not know know"), I believe that "not-knowing" (*pu chih*) is the author's way of saying "not intellectualizing," "not analyzing"—a meditative or semi-meditative exalted *state of awareness* that transcends knowledge, transcends distinctions, transcends thought. In the martial arts, for example, it enables one to anticipate, counter, and execute moves without thinking about them. Tennis players refer to it as "The Zone." In that state of mind, everything becomes *effortless*, *clear*, and *simple*. There is no *trying*. It produces the doing-without-doing simplicity that I believe martial-arts genius Bruce Lee was referring to when he said (in my favorite saying) that "Simplicity is the last step of art [meaning *artifice* or *technique*] and the beginning of nature."

In contrast, "to not know knowing"—if I followed the author's way of thinking and use of characters—refers to a *state of ignorance*, a limiting state in which one cannot accurately perceive, judge, or understand.

So my version of the first four lines of the above became: "To know *not-knowing* is the highest state. To not know *knowing* is a defect. Only those who know that that defect is a defect are accordingly without it."

My interpretation of the remainder of the text—which I believe was added by someone who was *not* a minimalist-word-game player—is: "The wise are without the defect because they know that the defect is a defect, and are accordingly without it." (My literal translation with two words added was: "Wise men not defective because they [know] defect [is] defect thus accordingly not defective.")

The typical English-language interpretation of this chapter is based on the interpretation of *ping* ("sickness," "defect," "fault ") as "sickness," which produces the following basic reading of the characters of the last five lines of the above: "Only men sick [of] sickness [are] thus accordingly not sick. Wise men [are] not sick because they [are] sick [of] sickness, thus accordingly [are] not sick." I doubt that the author was silly enough to believe that *only* those who are sick of sickness are not sick, or that someone sick of sickness is therefore not sick. I believe he was writing on a much higher level of meaning.

My theory—which of course cannot be proven unless and until the original is found—is that a not-very-perceptive copyist, having interpreted *ping* as "sick" and "sickness," removed as a mistake the character *chih* ("know, knowing") from between *fu* ("men") and *wei* ("only") in the text of the third line given above (in English, the three characters would have meant "only men knowing") and then added the characters that make up the text of the final three translated lines. The redundant characters of those final lines—which are redundant no matter how one interprets *ping*—are his "fingerprints."

72.
THE WISE RULER

> When the people do not respect
> A figure of authority,
> Then a greater figure of authority
> Will appear—
> One without a disdain for their
> Dwellings
> And without a loathing for their
> Livelihoods.

My translation of the text of the above:

> [When] the people not fear/dread/respect/be in awe of majesty/
> imposing/imperious/power/terror/awe then great/greater majesty/
> imposing/imperious/power/terror/awe arrive without disrespecting
>   their that-which-[they]-inhabit without loathing their that-by-
> which-[they]-live [.]

My generic version of other interpretations of the characters: "When the people no longer fear the one in power, then a great terror [or "what they greatly fear" or "a greater power"] will arrive. Do not scorn the places in which they live. Do not interfere with their means of livelihood."

As the above shows, other translators/interpreters interpret the third character, *wei*, as "fear" (in my line one, "respect") and apparently because of that interpret a different *wei*, "majesty/imposing," etc. (in my line two, "figure of authority") as signifying a fear-provoking tyrant who will in turn be replaced by an even greater evil. But the characters of my lines five through eight conflict with their interpretations. So they change the character-meaning "without" (*wu*) to "do not" (*pu*), replacing the conclusion of the author's opening thought with "do not" directives. But from whom are those directives coming? To whom are they addressed? Are they meant as warnings to the new tyrannical ruler?

All of that shows what happens when the interpreter starts out by seizing on one character-definition (typically because previous interpreters chose it) and then sticks with it to the end, regardless of what is encountered along the way.

"Ruler" in the first line of my second stanza and the first line of my third stanza is my substitute for the text's *fu*, "man," "master," or (more appropriately) "the one in question" in the first case and *jên*, "man," in the second. In each case, "ruler" seemed consistent with the contents of the first stanza's text, unlike "man"—the popular choice—which sends what's being said in another direction, making other versions of my second and third stanzas unrelated to the chapter's opening statement. Someone else, I found, thought as I did—James Legge: "In paragraph 4 [my third stanza], 'the sage' [*shêng jên*, "wise man"] must be 'the ruler who is a sage.'"

"High-price" in the fourth line of my third stanza is my in-that-context interpretation of *kuei*, "valuable," "costly, dear."

"Empties" in the third stanza's fifth line is from *chü*, a picture of a vessel with its lid removed, originally meaning "empty," "to empty," "to remove," but now meaning "to leave, to go," "past," "gone."

73.
THE NET OF HEAVEN

The Chinese text of my first stanza's two opening lines is *yang yü kan tsai sha*, which translates as:

> bravery/courage   in/through   daring/boldness   in accordance with a rule cuts/shears/slays/kills

Which results elsewhere in interpretations along the lines of: "A brave man who dares will kill," "Those who are brave in daring will be killed," and many variations of these—not one of which has ever made sense to me.

In researching the above characters, I learned that the ancient ancestor of the statement's third character, *kan* ("daring, boldness"), depicted a hand whipping a bear. I wondered if in ancient times *kan* had had any meanings in addition to "daring, boldness." Its picture, it seemed to me, suggested *violence*. I considered the text of lines five through seven, which asserts that heaven *detests* whatever-*kan*-meant. It seemed highly doubtful that heaven would detest mere daring or boldness. Also, how can there be such a thing as (in line three) bravery acting through non-*boldness*, or non-*daring*? Bravery by its very nature is bold, daring. Substituting "violence" for "daring" or "boldness" in lines one and three, I discovered that the chapter's opening statements suddenly made sense after all.

The point of this chapter seems to be that men's beliefs and behavior are not necessarily the same as heaven's—what some excessively *yang* men consider heroic and exciting, *yin* heaven considers foolish and destructive. Ultimately and inevitably, whatever the violent may believe or hope, judgment of all their harmful actions will be carried out, made possible by the soul-catching efficiency of the net of heaven, from which nothing, and no one, escapes.

74.
TAKING THE PLACE

All English-language interpretations that I've seen of my first stanza's lines four through ten go something like this: "If the people were to live in constant fear of death, and someone were to break the law and be executed, who would dare to break the law?" Such statements have the author supporting the belief of tyrannical rulers that applying the most extreme form of punishment would keep the people law-abiding—which conflicts with the caution he gives in the second stanza. To me, the first stanza is saying that repressive governments straitjacket their people, suppressing independent thought and self-expression.

The character that other interpretations of the chapter present as "break the law," "in an unlawful manner," and so on is *ch'i*, "extraordinary," "marvelous," "wonderful," "mysterious," "unusual," "strange." Those definitions seemed to me to have nothing to do with law-breaking. I found a literal analysis of *ch'i*, which said: "That which causes men to exclaim in admiration." The character is made up of *ta*, "great," etc. (a man stretching out his arms) and *k'o*, "to express admiration" (a mouth and a breath of warm approval)—which signifies *great expression[s] of admiration by one or more people*. So I interpreted *ch'i* as "In a manner acclaimed by the people" (lines six, seven, and ten).

Below is my character-by-character translation of the text of lines four through ten of the first stanza, with my interpretation of each section in parentheses. As have most previous interpreters of this chapter, I eliminated the "I" (*wu*) in what follows, as it didn't seem to belong there—nor did any other *wu* listed in classical dictionaries. Including the "I" results in wording such as: "I could grasp and kill" "I could be grasped and killed," "I could grasp and kill them," or—using an ancient meaning of *chih*—"I could grasp and kill *then* [my emphasis]." I ended up concluding that *chih*, in that ancient definition, is the beginning character of the next sentence. For the nonsensical *wu*, "I," which seemed to have taken the place of a character that *did* belong there, I substituted *k'o*, "can," "can be," "could," "could be":

> if made the people constantly fear death (If they were made to constantly fear death,) then acted admiration-inspiring one who (then anyone who acted in a manner acclaimed by the people) I [replaced in my version] obtained grasped and killed (could be seized and

put to death.) then who? dare (Then who would dare to act in a manner acclaimed by the people?)

The reason why "the people do not fear death" in the first stanza's first line is given in the next chapter.

Regarding "The Great Blade-Wielder" (*ta chiang*) in lines six and eight of my second stanza: *Chiang* depicts an axe and a hollowed-out log, and is defined as "artisan" (a bit tame for this context, I thought). *Ta chiang*, The Great Artisan (or Great Blade-Wielder) is The Way of Heaven.

Relative to the chapter's first stanza: In Bejing's Tiananmen Square in 1989 occurred the June Fourth Massacre, in which the People's Republic of China perpetrated the mass murder and attempted mass murder of thousands of men, women, and children. The Communist government, which officially claimed that only "around three hundred" people were killed in its destruction of the highly popular Democracy Movement, made the true death count impossible to determine. Who now will "dare to act in a manner acclaimed by the people"?

The second stanza describes another dilemma: the one facing those who will sooner or later topple China's totalitarian government. According to information passed on to me, the signs of an upcoming revolution in China are increasing in number. The government's time is running out. It would be wise for revolutionaries to remember that, as the *Tao Te Ching*'s author points out in the previous chapter, heaven detests bravery acting through violence, and the net of heaven will pull in all of those who destroy the lives of others. Those well-intentioned people who destroy the destroyers—the Communists—will not escape the net of heaven.

Perhaps the answer to that dilemma can be found in the *Tao Te Ching:* the superior power of *yin* energy. Instead of following the *yang* path of violence—which historically in China has tended to either rebound on and defeat revolutionaries or put the wrong people in power—maybe it's time to try another path. Maybe it's time to "fight fire with water" and in so doing honor the man who pointed out and defined "the way of the wise"—not merely honor him with lip service as the "Old Master" of questionable legend, and not merely honor him with prayers and incense as Lao-chün, the "Sovereign Master Lao" of Taoist religion, but instead honor him with *yin* action as the man who came up with a workable—and by now time-proven—alternative to brutality and destruction.

75.
THOSE ABOVE

"Increasingly" in the first and third lines of each of my first three stanzas is from ancient definitions of the text's *chih*—"grow, develop," "continue, progress."

I reworded the final sentence of each of my first three stanzas, which in my translation said: "Because of that, [they] starve" (first stanza); "Because of that, [they are] difficult [to] govern" (second stanza); and "Because of that, [they] think lightly of death" (third stanza).

Regarding my final stanza: Every English-language version of this chapter that I consulted had a different interpretation of the characters. I took that fact as a warning of difficulty ahead. After the usual translation work, I had the following, complete except for two characters: "Only those without [the] use [of] life act *chê shih* better than [to] value living."

Chê means "one who," "those who," "that which," etc. and originally could act as a connector. It clearly didn't belong in that statement. Having sometimes in this project confused *chê* at first glance with *jo* ("resembles," "like," "as," "as if," or "if"), I thought that a copyist might have done the same. I decided to try substituting the latter character for the former, choosing the definition "as if." That produced: "Only those without [the] use [of] life act as if *shih* better than [to] value living." That seemed promising, so I turned to *shih*.

Shih translates as "this," "that," "thus," or "right, correct." In context, only "that"— referring to "think lightly of death" in the previous stanza—made sense: "Only those without [the] use [of] life act as if that [is] better than [to] value living."

76.
THE DISCIPLES

Unlike most of the chapters, this one revealed to me no surprises. What's notable about it is the depth of thought behind it, pointing out as it does the vulnerability of the big and powerful, the hard and unyielding. As the saying goes, "The bigger they are, the harder they fall." Our bigger-is-better society has in recent years begun to give some attention to that message. Maybe it now can give some more attention to the chapter's other message: that "the pliant and tender"—the flexible and yielding, "the disciples of life"—point the way to future survival.

The chapter's two messages can be verified by the dead dinosaurs (who are saying nothing about it) and their small, mobile, surviving descendants, the birds (who are saying a great deal about it).

77.
HEAVEN'S WAY
THE WISE II

As a former back-property archer, I would say that the comparison the author makes in the text of my first section's first stanza implies that he likely was an archer. I modified the generic wording of the text of the stanza's last three lines—which may have been made generic by copyists—in order to complete the "picture" that seemed to have been intended.

The text of lines four through nine of the second stanza, though written around 2,400 years ago, sums up our situation today at the hands of our own era's "rob-and-boasters."

The last line of the second stanza is my interpretation of the text's *wei* ("only") *yu* ("has") *tao* ("The Way") *chê* ("one who"). Other interpretations I've seen say "Only one who has the Way," or an equivalent—which, to me, makes the author seem bigoted: "Who is able to have an abundance to offer to the world? Only one who has the Way." That missionary zeal does not seem the author's style. (Anti-Confucianism is one thing; bigotry is another.) From the character-order and my reading of the author and the text, I believe that what's being said is that someone who only has The Way, even though he has nothing else, has more of what the world needs than have the excessively cluttered wealthy, who have everything but what matters. In my reading, the author does not mean to imply that *only* one who only has The Way has more to offer to the world.

A point of interest: The character *hou*, "[feudal-era] prince," in both its ancient and brush-written forms consists of the picture of an arrow, a target, and a man.

78.
THE SOFT AND THE HARD
RESPONSIBILITY

Regarding the word *attacking* (from *kung*, "to attack") in the third line of my first stanza: Water is the gentlest power in nature, and is therefore the most likely to be underestimated. But when it attacks, it *attacks*. In its own way. It doesn't behave like *yang* energy: It doesn't flex muscles, it doesn't draw out a dangerous weapon—it just *flows*, carrying all before it without effort.

In response to any argument about which is the greater power, *yin* or *yang*, I would say: Water can conquer fire; fire cannot conquer water.

The chapter's second section seems related to the author's previously stated theme that the greatest rulers and leaders are *yin* in their behavior—modest, non-egocentric, ruling and leading by encouraging their people rather than by glorifying themselves, giving credit to others for work done. Here the author is saying that those who take upon themselves the responsibility of dealing with the most lowly and difficult problems-of-state are the ones best qualified to be at the head of a government—and the more such responsibility they accept, the higher they can rise.

In ancient China, every state had shrines to the agriculture-spirits, those of grain (*shê*) and crops (*chi*). A state's king could be referred to, as the author does in the text of line four, as *shê chi chu*, "Grain [and] Crops Lord," which for clarity I rendered as "Lord of the Land."

Unlike other translators/interpreters, I interpreted *kuo* in the context of its first appearance (line three) as "state" and in the context of its second appearance (line six) as "nation."

While going over this chapter "one last time"—as I would say before going over a chapter three or four more times—I received the impression that when he'd written it, the author had been working on a plan to achieve the society-changes he wanted to see, by applying the power and tactics of water that he'd learned from his observations. That was all—just a quick impression, and then it was gone.

In our extremely y*ang*-skewed, cowboy/tomboy society, which considers exaggerated masculine values the only values worth considering—in which brutal, brainless behavior is a standard feature of "entertainment"; in which many boys and men are conditioned to believe that compassion and regard for others (men, women, children, animals) are signs of weakness; in which "equality for women" is increasing admiration for *yang* women far more than for *yin* women; in which a woman is called a "strong woman" only when she is strong like a man; and in which many who label themselves "feminists" could more accurately and honestly label themselves "masculinists"—the *yin*-favoring wisdom of the *Tao Te Ching* will not easily be understood, respected, or put into practice. But any society that ignores the practical, life-supporting advantages of *yin* energy does so at its own peril.

America's alarming shootings-statistics show that our pathologically *yang* society, like a diseased organism, is attacking itself. Shooting victims range from defenseless children to some of the finest leaders and progress-builders the world has ever known—courageous people who made a huge positive difference, until they were gunned down. And then the progress stopped. As the late renowned Chicago columnist Mike Royko put it, "No other country kills so many of its best people." And kills so much of a better future in the process. As of December 2018, Americans own more than three hundred million firearms. More than 4.5 million American children (2019) have access to loaded, unlocked guns in their homes. In 2019, gunshot wounds were the third leading cause of death to American children. In 2018, approximately 4,200 loaded firearms—an increase of 70 percent over the previous year—were discovered by American airport security personnel in carry-on luggage, often packed with spare magazines or cartridges. According to a recent report on that trend, the numbers from July 2019–July 2020 were three times higher than for the previous twelve-month period. Airport security forces have stated that even more carry-on guns are probably getting by undetected.

The existence in America of more than one thousand hate organizations (2018) and what the late author Toni Morrison called in a watchdog-organization newsletter "the explosive growth of armed militias and conspiracy minded antigovernmental groups" indicates how dangerously *yang* our nation has become. Our growing assaults on each other are overtaxing our law-enforcement agencies and overfilling our prisons. And our ongoing assaults on nature are sealing our fate. Nature, as always, will have the final word. And it should by now be clear to anyone of intelligence what that final word will be: When we have driven the Valley Spirit away, what remains will be *death*.

79.
OBLIGATIONS

In ancient China, a contract of obligation between a debtor and a creditor was written on two halves of a bamboo slip. The debtor retained the left half; the creditor retained the right half. When the debt was paid, the two halves were joined, dissolving the obligation. As in other societies old and new, a debtor might dispute the terms of the agreement, pressure the creditor to change a part of it, or file charges against the creditor—or simply refuse to live up to the contract terms. In this chapter's example, the two parties strongly resent each other at the beginning of the agreement. So, to prevent an even more unpleasant situation from developing, the author recommends that the debtor not spin the wheel of retribution—that he behave himself and not play the dispute-the-agreement game. *Wei wu wei*—make life easier.

Many English-language interpretations (but not the standard text) have the author's "wise man" holding the *right* half of the contract-slip, making him the creditor who does not push for repayment of the debt. But to me, the chapter is about meeting obligations, not about letting people evade them. Therefore, the wise man holding the debtor's half seemed more reasonable to me than the alternative. Besides, it follows the characters.

In my first stanza, I added "listing his obligations" (ninth line).

In my final stanza, I added "obligations to" (second line). The text of that stanza, *t'ien tao wu ch'in ch'ang yü shan jên*, translates as:

heaven way without a relative/kindred [therefore] constantly/
consistently gives to/shares with good man/men

The usual interpretation of the characters goes something like: "The Way is impartial, it is always with the good man"—which to me is a contradiction. The following is my explanation of what the characters seem to be saying:

In ancient times, China's nobility / upper class was a society of powerful clans—and consequently a society of compelling obligations to powerful clan members. In the granting of favors and patronage, relatives came first, outsiders came second (if at all). I believe the author is humorously saying that The Way has no relatives (no Cousin Wong, no Auntie Wu), and therefore has no family obligations—so it is free to choose whom to favor. And it chooses to consistently favor the good.

On the subject of humor, consider the sly dig that I made into my second stanza: "Has-Virtue manages [his] agreements. Without-Virtue manages [the collection of] tax"—a remark worthy of Charles Dickens.

Many have commented on the seeming lack of logic in the sequence of chapters in the *Tao Te Ching*. However, if one considers the possibility that the work was written at leisure as a diary, some logic in its thought-progression can be seen: The latter part of the previous chapter concerns responsibility, so this chapter is about the related subject of meeting obligations; Chapter Thirty concerns the rebounding of military force, and is followed by a chapter on war; and so on. From that pattern, one could deduce that the related-subject pairs or larger groupings were likely composed at one sitting—although some at least were likely refined later—while the isolated-subject chapters were likely composed at separate times. And regarding deductions:

Most of the chapters from Chapter Sixty-Eight onward are shorter and simpler than most of the chapters preceding them—which could suggest that toward the end of the work, the author was running short of writing time, opportunities, or energy.

80.
DELETED

Years ago, when I first read an English-language version of the *Tao Te Ching*, my reaction to Chapter Eighty was that its return-to-the-old-days theme didn't fit in with the rest of the chapters. Now, having translated the chapter's characters, I believe that its writing is the work of another author.

The wording is extremely simple, but not the same sort of extremely simple as is found in the great majority of the other chapters—it is *plain and ordinary* simple, not *sophisticated* simple. To make an analogy, it's like a basic, rustic chair as opposed to a Scandinavian Modern chair. Its statements are just *statements*—matter-of-fact, normal writing lacking the creativity of the author of the *Tao Te Ching*. Ironically, perhaps intentionally, it seems far more in line with the Lao-tzŭ legend than do the other chapters, as it consists of the sort of backward-looking musings that the disillusioned "Old Master" would likely have left on his way out of what was to become known as China. Its attitude seems that of an old man, while to me the attitude of the great majority of chapters seems that of a young man.

Writings are like fingerprints—they reveal the individuality of whoever left them.

81.
SINCERE WORDS
THE WISE II
THE WAY OF THE WISE

During the declining years of the Chou Dynasty, especially the final part of it that began shortly after Master K'ung's death, a great number of philosophers appeared in the "Center Nation," each claiming to have the philosophy to (depending on the individual philosophy-school's focus) benefit rulers, reunify the nation, or counter the disintegration of society. Of the era's Hundred Schools of philosophy, only the two of broadest vision, Confucianism and Taoism, survived the succeeding centuries.

In what I've made the first section of this chapter, the author appears to be dismissing the flattery, bickering, and superficial knowledge that he sees in the behavior of at least some of the Hundred-Schools philosophers, primarily (by his wording) the Confucianists.

In the two final lines of that first section, the author distinguishes between *chih*, "knowing," "perception," or "wisdom," and *po*, "wide knowledge." The usual interpretation of the text is: "The wise are not learned; the learned are not wise." But that's a misleading representation of what the characters are saying.

Master K'ung worked diligently to acquire *po*, "wide knowledge"—a term that will always be associated with him—and urged his followers to do the same. In contrast, the author of the *Way Virtue Classic* favored what might be called *deep* knowledge—that which could be gained through observation, deduction, and reflection, particularly concerning the earthly actions of the greatest power of heaven and earth and the knowledge of how best to emulate them. Master K'ung did not concern himself with matters of nature or spirit, and he expressed doubt that appeals made to *t'ien* ("Sky" or "Heaven"), his era's name for the divine universal power, could have any possible effect. (So why, one might ask, did he prescribe all those religious rituals?) Consequently, from the viewpoint of the *Tao Te Ching*'s author, and of countless Taoists after him, the teachings of Master K'ung and his followers, for all their supposed concern with "wide knowledge," had gaping holes in them. (For example, the natural sciences in China—including anatomy and medicine—have always been the province of Taoists rather than Confucianists.) As later became all too evident, Confucian "wide knowledge" information-gathering perpetuated a sheltered and isolated, backward-looking, halls-of-power view honoring and imitating former rulers, statesmen, writers, and wise men while largely ignoring the present everyday needs of the majority of people. And when it came to serving those people, Confucian "wide knowledge," rules, and rituals made poor substitutes for vision, substance, and sincerity. So it's not *knowledge* that the author is dismissing, or what *we* would consider "wide knowledge" to be—it's *the kind of knowledge advocated by the Confucianists.*

In the text of the first line of my second section, the author, I believe, means more by *chi*, "accumulate," than merely "store up material goods." One can accumulate knowledge, beneficial life lessons, and other educational advantages and keep them to oneself. Or one can accumulate them in order to become a well-known, well-endorsed philosophy master with power over the less-educated, the less-thoughtful. Or one can do as the author advocates at the end of the stanza: Give them to others.

THE PHOTOGRAPHS: THE VALLEY SPIRIT

The photographs in this book are from my file of Kodachrome transparencies, all taken in Oregon with an Olympus OM-1 35mm camera using either a 50mm macro lens, a 28mm wide angle, or a 200mm telephoto. All images were printed unmanipulated and uncropped.

I consider Kodachrome (now discontinued) and Fujichrome Velvia professional transparency film (when used with a warming filter for a Kodachrome look) the best for capturing images of nature, due to their natural tone, their rich saturation, their ability to reproduce minute color differences, and their fine grain. For my purposes, those films are far superior to the digital format. Nature, I believe, deserves to be portrayed as she appears to the human eye and brain, with all of her color subtleties and variations intact, rather than with the gaudy, simplistic "makeup" of digital color—autumn leaves all the same overbright yellow, blades of grass all the same overbright green—that turns natural landscapes into unnatural landscapes. Fine-grain film is nature's faithful mirror.

Notes on Selected Images

Page 11: Taken at the top of Saddle Mountain, in the Oregon Coast Range, as fog crept across the depression between the peaks. On a clear day, one can from there look east to the Cascade Range, look north up the coast to the mouth of the Columbia River, or in places—with caution—look straight down for more than three thousand feet. During the Ice Age, Saddle Mountain was high enough to enable flowers to survive that can't be found at lower elevations.

Pages 2, 26, 45: Not the mountains of China, but the monoliths of the Columbia River Gorge, near Dodson, Oregon. This mysterious, deeply wooded section of the Gorge, near the western end of the 1,200-mile-long "Mighty Columbia"—written and sung about by Woody Guthrie—is known as "the Gateway."

Pages 75, 78, 121: Oneonta Gorge is a mini-gorge ("slot canyon") running into the river at a right angle. Three of its features: flowers and other plants said to exist nowhere else in the world; strange holes formed in its rock walls around sixteen million years ago; and a hidden waterfall.

More waterfalls can be found in the western end of the Gorge than in any similar-size area in the lower forty-eight states.

Dedicated on June 7, 1916, Oregon's Historic Columbia River Highway through the Gorge was the creation of a number of right people in the right place at the right time, including a financial backer who was both far-seeing visionary and rock-steady practical, the newly created Oregon State Highway Commission, supportive Multnomah County officials, a team of Italian stone masons, and a nature-loving, award-winning, innovative-genius highway engineer—all of whom resonated emotionally and spiritually with the haunting beauty of the Gorge. June 7, 2016, marked the internationally acclaimed, internationally visited highway's centennial.

Today, however, most of the twenty-five Columbia Gorge scenes in this book could not be photographed.

In 2017, after the above descriptions were written—two weeks before the coming of the September rains that would end the hottest, driest Oregon summer then on record—an out-of-state fifteen-year-old with no regard for nature or the many warnings of extreme fire danger threw two smokebombs into a wooded ravine in the Gorge, starting a fire later described by an observer as "Hell on Earth." The high wall of flame advanced rapidly, with the wind hurling embers a mile or more ahead of it, touching off smaller fires that were soon engulfed by the moving inferno. Towns and communities in the Gorge were evacuated—East Corbett, Warrendale, Dodson, Larch Mountain, Latourell, Bridal Veil, Cascade Locks, parts of Troutdale—as the fire swept on, coming close to the town of Hood River on the east and the outskirts of Portland on the west before the winds shifted. An air-quality expert declared Portland's smoke-filled air to be "worse than Beijing's." A few areas near the Historic Highway survived with comparatively little damage, thanks to fire-fighting crews from all over the state and the high humidity of what I call the "tourist falls." But the nearly one thousand firefighters were unable to stop the major part of the blaze, which was only declared "fully contained"—although it was still burning, despite the rain—on November 30.

My favorite part of the Gorge, the deep, mysterious wooded hills and ravines beyond the tourist falls—shown in part in the three monoliths-in-fog photographs in this book—was visually ruined in some places, totally destroyed in others. In the latter, pathetic-looking trails wander through a war-zone-like landscape populated by black standing and fallen poles that once were trees. Gone are the residents of the forest—incinerated, mostly—including the friendly chipmunks I would encounter who could brighten any day. Many areas were so badly burned that they will not be able to regenerate themselves, and will therefore need to be human-replanted.

After the fire came the second stage of destruction. Since all of the vegetation in many areas had been burned away in the inferno, including the roots and thick mosses that had held the rocks of the hillsides in place, huge rockslides and landslides injured the Gorge still further. In the Oneonta Gorge area, for example, so many rocks fell after the fire that the ground could hardly be glimpsed. More rocks will be falling, say the experts—for years.

As of this writing, three years after the fire, what remains of most of Oregon's former "crown jewel" is more than fifty thousand acres of damage and destruction. As the judge pointed out when sentencing the fire-starter, it will take *generations* for the Gorge to recover. In my opinion, a large amount of it will never be an equivalent of what it was. The fate of the area's businesses, most of which have depended on visitor-patronage, has yet to be determined.

In the meantime, rockslides, landslides, and falling trees are still cluttering or obliterating trails, the Historic Highway, and the surrounding areas as one of nature's irreplaceable masterpieces breaks apart.

As a sad testament to human insensitivity to nature, most of the scenes in this book could not be photographed today because of human-caused fire, clear-cut logging, and "development."

Pages 55, 72, 91: A stream in Portland's Forest Park, the largest urban forest in America (5,157 acres), which is connected by a wildlife corridor to the Oregon Coast Range. The Chinese-style pottery jar in the photograph for Chapter Fifteen is one I made.

Page 128: My parents' badminton court in winter frost, Sylvan. The vase is from my father's collection of Asian pottery. Leaving no discernible footprints in the brittle, frosty grass was a test of Taoist light-footedness ("A skilled walker leaves no tracks"). This photograph and the one accompanying Chapter Fifteen are from my college graduation-thesis presentation.

Had it not been for the influence of my father's East/West background and approach to life, my love of nature that began in the woods of Sylvan (now mostly destroyed), and my longstanding fascination with codes and ciphers, this book would not have come into existence.

The General Locations of the Scenes Photographed

The Columbia River Gorge National Scenic Area: pages 2, 8-9, 13, 14, 22, 26, 36, 42, 45, 49, 56, 60, 64, 75, 78, 84, 88, 92, 105, 110, 117, 121, 125, 139, 142
Saddle Mountain State Natural Area: pages 10, 63
Silver Falls State Park: pages 46, 132
Forest Park: pages 55, 72, 91
Ecola State Park: pages 67, 136
Oregon coast: pages 19, 81, 95, 100
Sylvan: pages 50, 59, 128
Private garden, Portland: page 87

Editor: Elizabeth Broussard
Managing Editor: Annalea Manalili
Designer: Darilyn Lowe Carnes
Production Manager: Anet Sirna-Bruder

Library of Congress Control Number: 2021932552

ISBN: 978-1-4197-5550-7
eISBN: 978-1-64700-361-6

Abrams books are available at special discounts when purchased in quantity for premiums and promotions as well as fundraising or educational use. Special editions can also be created to specification. For details, contact specialsales@abramsbooks.com or the address below.

Abrams® is a registered trademark of Harry N. Abrams, Inc.

ABRAMS The Art of Books
195 Broadway, New York, NY 10007
abramsbooks.com